Medieval Iconography and Narrative

A Symposium

Odense University Press · 1980

Proceedings of the Fourth International Symposium
organized by the
Centre for the Study of Vernacular Literature
in the Middle Ages.
Held at Odense University
on 19-20 November, 1979.

Edited by
Flemming G. Andersen
Esther Nyholm
Marianne Powell
Flemming Talbo Stubkjær

1980 by Odense University Press
OAB-Tryk, Odense
ISBN 87 7492 307 2

Trykt med støtte fra Odense Universitet.
Anbefalet til udgivelse af lektor Inger-Lise Kolstrup
og adjunktvikar Hans Jørgen Frederiksen.

Contents

Preface

The Symposium on Medieval Iconography and Narrative was held on 19-20 November 1979 at Odense University. This was the fourth international Symposium organized by the *Centre for the Study of Vernacular Literature in the Middle Ages,* and this year's Chairman was Flemming Talbo Stubkjær. We wish to express our thanks to Odense University and to the Danish Research Council for the Humanities for the support that made it possible to arrange the Symposium and to publish these proceedings. The papers are here presented in the order in which they were read.

Further acknowledgements are due to Bibliothèque Nationale, Paris; Bild-archiv d. Öst. Nationalbibliothek; Bodleian Library, Oxford; The British Library, London; Gab. fotografico, Soprintendenza beni artistici e storici di Firenze; Manx Museum, Douglas, Isle of Man; Photographie Bulloz, Paris; Service Photographique, Paris; and thanks to Pat Banham for the drawings accompanying Dr Margeson's paper.

The Editors

Introduction

by MARIANNE POWELL

Eight speakers were invited to read papers at the Symposium, but unfortunately two of them had to withdraw owing to ill health, Professor Wolfgang Brückner of the University of Würzburg, who was to have given the opening lecture, and Professor Elizabeth Salter of the University of York. Dr Susan Margeson, Castle Museum Norwich, kindly accepted an invitation to give a paper in place of Professor Brückner, and Professor Derek Pearsall of the University of York offered to substitute for Elizabeth Salter and to deliver his version of the same lecture, as the two scholars had worked closely together on the subject for some years. Hence the paper read by Professor Pearsall is published under joint authorship.

In May 1980 came the unhappy news of Elizabeth Salter's death, which in spite of her long illness was a profound shock to her friends and colleagues. Elizabeth Salter's contributions to medieval studies are well-known. She played a leading part in the foundation of the *Centre for Medieval Studies* at the University of York in 1970 and was its Director until 1978, her dynamic personality and enthusiasm for establishing new projects playing a very substantial part in its success. In her books and articles she has left further testimony to her versatile talents and scholarship, in which breadth of vision is always combined with depth and sensitivity. The Medieval Centre at York is an interdisciplinary institution, and much of Elizabeth Salter's work, especially in recent years, was concerned with the relationship between literature and the pictorial arts, a subject to which she devoted herself with energy and inspiration. Elizabeth Salter's untimely death is a great personal loss and a loss to medieval scholarship.

The subject of the Symposium at Odense, Medieval Iconography and Narrative, calls for some introductory comments. It was abundantly clear to the delegates, as it also appears from the collection of papers published in this volume, that not everyone understands the same thing by the concepts of iconography and narrative. For the purposes of the conference, however, they were taken in their widest sense, and this explains the diversity of material offered. The diversity has proved to be particularly valuable as it can be seen that scholars working on very different materials, with different methods, and even different interpretations of the key concepts, arrive at similar results concerning some of the basic problems in the relationship between literary and pictorial representations.

Thus Dr Esther Nyholm in her paper on Petrarch's *Triumphs* and Professor Pearsall in his study of the Chaucer Frontispiece focus on a similar question of discrepancy between text and illustration, and Derek Pearsall shows that an answer may be found in the study of workshop practice and workshop repertoires of stock motifs and iconographical models. As in the case of the Chaucer Frontispiece the nature of the illustrations to Petrarch's *Triumphs* may be explained by the use of established pictorial models.

Derek Pearsall's argument that workshop practice has important things to teach the literary scholar has wide ramifications, as was clear from the subsequent discussion of his paper. The idea that religious iconographical models could be transferred to secular texts without a necessary transfer of religious meaning shakes the foundations of Robertsonianism, and the point made that it was sometimes quite insignificant scenes in a narrative that were illustrated simply because the iconography for these already existed warns us against using illustrations as a safe guide to an understanding of the contemporary way of reading a narrative. Finally, the existence of workshop repertoires may determine the use of certain literary works in decoration without necessarily proving popularity for the work itself. The existence of numerous carvings of a limited number of scenes from the *Roman de Renart* on the misericords of English churches was mentioned in the discussion as a case in point.

The pre-existence of iconographical models in a very different context was considered by Dr Heinrich Beck in his paper on Wayland the Smith. Dr Beck traced the development of the Germanic fable of Wayland the artisan into Wayland the artist and showed how this was caused by a fusion of this figure with famous artists of the classical world such as Apelles, Daedalus, Alexander and Icarus. The fusion was accomplished to a large extent by an adoption of the ancient iconography for these figures, and subsequently the iconography came to influence the narrative and change its perspective.

The transfer of iconography was discussed by Dr Susan Margeson in her paper on the Vǫlsung legend in medieval art. Susan Margeson illustrated the dangers of careless methods of identification and in the interpretation of her own material she carefully avoids unfounded assumptions. The fact that the Vǫlsung legend was used in Christian contexts, Dr Margeson argues, does not necessarily suggest a Christian allegorization of the legend. If religious iconography can be transferred to a secular context without a transfer of religious meaning (as Derek Pearsall argued) the converse may also be true. The depiction of Gunnar in the snake pit on a carved baptismal font mentioned by Susan Margeson was taken up in the discussion following her paper, and the discussion showed how widely scholars differ in their readiness to attribute allegorical meaning to pagan themes employed in Christian religious contexts. While for some the death symbolism of Gunnar in the pit easily paired with the Pauline phrases of the baptismal liturgy ("in baptism we die with Christ to rise again in him") others interpreted the figure as a parallel to Jonas and thus saw him as a resurrection figure, while others again preferred to stress its purely decorative function.

The problem of deciding the presence or absence of allegorical meaning is central to much present day discussion of both literature and art. One particular aspect of it, which did not form part of any of the papers of the Symposium but would have been very relevant to its theme, is the relationship between marginalia and main picture in illuminated manuscripts. Elizabeth Salter has devoted a great deal of attention to this subject and to the problem of deciding when marginalia relate allegorically to the main illustration, when they are more plausibly taken as an expression of horror vacui, as pure decoration, or the results of an artist's doodling. The fools discussed in Ulla Haastrup's paper (see below) present a similar problem. Should they be interpreted allegorically as part of the didactic scheme of the main illustrations or are they introduced by the artist to give a touch of local colour? And again, are they to be taken as a clear testimony of the connection between wall paintings and contemporary drama?

Two of the speakers at the Symposium had the advantage of being able to present their illustrative material in its original form instead of slides. The Symposium programme included a visit to the village church of Bellinge a few miles south west of Odense, and Knud Banning and Ulla Haastrup had been invited to give their papers on the fifteenth century wall paintings of Bellinge in the church itself. Dr Banning explained the pictures and discussed the problematic relationship between them and their source, the *Biblia Pauperum,* while Ulla Haastrup's paper was concerned with the relationship of the paintings to contemporary drama.

A lively discussion followed Dr Banning's paper, centring on the conflict between the two principles of representation, the chronological nature of the Passion narrative and the static typological oppositions, and on the problems this conflict creates for the instructional function of the paintings. Similar problems are of course known from other areas of church decoration – the Verdun altar immediately springs to mind – and one delegate argued persuasively that the two organic principles, chronology and typology, supported by the architectural structure of the building (the progressive narration is painted on the walls, the typological pairs in the cells of the vaults) formed a synthesis of a higher order.

The typological pairings in Bellinge show some confusion on the part of the painters, and Dr Banning showed that this was partly due to the problem of fitting the triple system of the *Biblia Pauperum* to the four cells of the vaults. He further suggested, however, that the availability of models may have been as important a consideration for the painters as the adherence to a typological tradition which they may not have understood, a point which again stresses the importance of workshop repertoires. The use of identical motifs in the wall paintings of different related churches was mentioned by Søren Kaspersen as a further indication of an established workshop. Søren Kaspersen made some weighty contributions to the discussion of the Bellinge paintings and was invited to put his arguments into written form for inclusion in the proceedings.

Ulla Haastrup's paper discusses some of the conventions in late Gothic wall painting and takes up the classic problem of the reciprocal influence of wall paintings and mystery plays. For Danish wall paintings the problem is particularly difficult since no texts of Danish plays have survived. The texts of contemporary English, French and German plays may help to elucidate certain problems in the paintings, as for example the representation of Simon of Cyrene as a peasant, which Ulla Haastrup suggests may be due to the mystery plays, which often use Simon as a voice of social complaint. The introduction of the famous fools in the Bellinge paintings (already referred to) may be similarly explained. To the more general problem of the existence and direction of influence between the dramatic and pictorial representations Ulla Haastrup retains an open mind, but suggests the possibility of a common origin for them both. The possible identity of such an origin was not discussed, but scholars have of course already produced candidates such as for example the *Dialogus S. Anselmi cum B.V. Maria* by Pseudo-Anselm and Pseudo-Bonaventura's *Meditationes Vitae Christi*. The study of how narrative treatises together with liturgical and paraliturgical texts were translated into a pictorial mode through a process of concretization of metaphors and similes has produced new theories which in an interesting way complement earlier ones. The abstract of Professor Brückner's introductory paper, which unfortunately had to be cancelled, had amongst other important themes promised a discussion of this process.

Professor Kurt Schier's paper, like Susan Margeson's concerns problems of identification, in particular the relationship between detail and whole, a problem not unrelated to the question of the connection between marginalia and main illustration. Professor Schier shows that frequently pictorial representations are identifiable only through a detail in the picture, and when the dates of the picture and the text adduced as identificatory material differ by as much as 500 years, the basic question arises how we choose the textual material which we want to use for the identification, and how we justify our choice. As the paper illustrates, a different choice of text is likely to produce a different interpretation, and sometimes details are interpretable though not the main composition, while sometimes the opposite is the case. Professor Schier raises a number of questions and reveals a number of pitfalls in order to illustrate his main argument, which concerns the necessity for interdisciplinary cooperation.

An excellent example of interdisciplinary research is offered by Professor Sixten Ringbom's paper on the art of reading pictorial narratives. Professor Ringbom gives a lucid exposition of various artistic conventions used for dealing with the problems of transforming narratives into visual terms, and shows how in the more successful illustrations different methods may combine to produce very subtle results. Professor Ringbom stresses the powerful and direct influence of literature on the visual arts in the middle ages, and like Kurt Schier he concludes that often a picture cannot be understood without the literary text to elucidate it. For the literary scholar in particular Professor Ringbom's paper provides a safe and useful guide to an understanding of pictorial vocabulary.

The Symposium on iconography and narrative in Odense proved a reaffirmation of the value of interdisciplinary approaches to problems of medieval art and literature. Attacking the problems from different angles the papers show that there is a great deal to be gained from the study of the interaction between the two modes of representation. Pitfalls abound, but ways to avoid some of them have been pointed out, particularly in the study of the working methods of medieval artists and workshops, and of the conventions they employ. Though in the medieval theology of art pictorial representation was considered subservient to the word, it is quite clear from the present studies that a dynamic relationship exists between the two art forms, and that the study of this relationship must take into account the particular problems besetting each mode and respect the integrity of both media.

Aarhus University

Der kunstfertige Schmied – ein ikonographisches und narratives Thema des frühen Mittelalters

von Heinrich Beck

Die Fabel vom kunstfertigen Schmied,[1] der nach grausamer Rache aus der Gefangenschaft eines Herrschers entflieht, ist in der germanischen Überlieferung gut dokumentiert – sowohl in literarischer als auch in ikonographischer Darstellung: angefangen von einem angelsächsischen Schmuckkästchen, dem sog. Franks Casket (um 700), dem gotländischen Bildstein von Ardre VIII mit seiner Schmiedeszene (aus dem 8. Jh.) bis zu den literarischen Denkmälern, der altenglischen „Deors Klage" (aufgezeichnet im Exeter Book, Ende des 10. Jhs.), der eddischen Vǫlundarkviða und der westnordischen Thidrekssaga (beide im 13. Jh. aufgezeichnet).

Die Forschungsinteressen der jüngsten Zeit galten unterschiedlichen Gesichtspunkten: den vor- und nachchristlichen ikonographischen Gestaltungen dieses Themas,[2] den sozialgeschichtlichen Aspekten der Schmiedefabel,[3] den literarischen Denkmälern in ihrer gegenseitigen Beziehung und zeitlichen Schichtung,[4] den Fragen eines Wechselverhältnisses von sprachlicher und bildlicher Darstellung.[5]

[1] Der Symposium-Beitrag stellt die Kurzfassung einer eingehenderen Untersuchung zum Thema des kunstfertigen Schmiedes im frühen Mittelalter dar. Die hier oftmals nur angedeutete Argumentation wird dort ausführlicher dargelegt.

[2] J. T. Lang, „Sigurd and Weland in Pre-Conquest Carving from Northern England". In: *The Yorkshire Archaeological Journal* 48, 1976, 83-94.

[3] K. Hauck, „Wielands Hort. Die sozialgeschichtliche Stellung des Schmiedes in frühen Bildprogrammen nach und vor dem Religionswechsel". In: *Kungl. Vitterhets Historie och Antikvitets Akademien. Antikvarisk Arkiv* 64, Stockholm 1977, 5-31.

[4] H. Schück, „ Vǫlundsagan". In: *ANF* 5, 1893, 103-117. S. Bugge, „Det oldnorske Kvad om Vǫlund (Vǫlundarkviða) og dets Forhold til engelske Sagn". In: *ANF* 26, 1910, 32-77. F. Panzer, „Zur Wielandsage". In: *Zeitschrift für Volkskunde,* Neue Folge II, Bde. 1/2, 1930, 125-135. G. Baesecke, „Die Herkunft der Wielanddichtung". In: *Beiträge zur Geschichte der deutschen Sprache und Literatur* 61, 1937, 368-378. J. de Vries, „Bemerkungen zur Wielandsage". In: *Edda, Skalden, Saga. FS für Felix Genzmer, hg. v. H. Schneider.* Heidelberg 1952, 173-199.

[5] A. Wolf, „Franks Casket in literarhistorischer Sicht". In: *Frühmittelalterliche Studien. Jahrbuch des Instituts für Frühmittelalterforschung der Universität Münster.* Hg. v. K. Hauck. Bd. 3, Berlin 1969, 227-243.

Es bestätigen diese Arbeiten, daß das Schmiedethema, das im Germanischen mit dem Namen Wieland (altnordisch Vǫlundr, altenglisch Welund) verbunden ist, einen weiten geographischen und zeitlichen Horizont einnimmt: Es ist auf dem Kontinent, in England und in Skandinavien bekannt, es reicht mindestens bis in das 7. Jh. zurück. Deutlich machen diese Arbeiten auch, daß in einer jahrhundertelangen Tradition die Fabel von der grausamen Rache des gefangenen Schmiedes in den Grundzügen bewahrt blieb – und doch gleichzeitig eine beachtliche Neigung zur Rezeption außergermanischen Erzählgutes bestand. Als Folge davon entstehen Varianten, deren Summe das Thema vom kunstfertigen und racheübenden Schmied ausmacht. Die Rezeptionsvorgänge und Variantenbildungen erfolgen in einem geschichtlichen Prozeß, der dichtungsgeschichtlich ebenso aufschlußreich wie historisch interessant ist. Die Gunst der Überlieferung ermöglicht es, die relativ späten literarischen Denkmäler in ihrem Variantenreichtum zu messen an bildlichen Quellen hohen Alters.

In der folgenden Darlegung wird versucht, neues und altertümliches Quellenmaterial in die Diskussion einzubeziehen und die Konsequenzen aus der hier angenommenen spätantik-germanischen Kontaktnahme zu ziehen.

Die narrativen Quellen: Rezeption und Erzählvarianten

Die literarischen Denkmäler, Vǫlundarkviða, Deors Klage, Wielandabschnitt der Thidrekssaga, stimmen darin überein, daß der kunstfertige Schmied rachenehmend einer Gefangenschaft bei einem König Níðuðr (altenglisch Nidhād) entflieht. Offensichtlich macht diese Rachefabel den Kern der Erzählung aus. Um diesen Kern lagert sich ein beweglicheres Erzählgut, das kompilierend angeschwellt (wie in der Thidrekssaga), knapp und andeutend gehalten sein konnte (wie in der Vǫlundarkviða). Einig ist die Forschung sich darin, daß die erweiterte Fabel weitgehend von der Rezeption außergermanischen Erzählgutes bestimmt ist – dem internationalen Wandergut von den drei Schwanenmädchen und dem antiken Erzählstoff vom exemplarischen Künstler (Daidalos, Apelles, Alexander). Wenig erörtert blieb in dieser Diskussion über Umfang, Art und Weg dieser Rezeption die Frage nach den Gründen: Wieso werden aus einem reichen Erzählrepertoire, das offenbar den spätantiken Erzählschatz einschloß, bestimmte Themen rezipiert, andere nicht. Welche Absichten bestimmten einen solchen Selektionsprozeß? Eine Antwort darauf könnte auch zum Verständnis der Kernfabel und der geschichtlichen Entwicklung des Wielandthemas insgesamt beitragen.

Narratives Lehngut ist dann relativ einfach zu bestimmen, wenn es als Fremdgut auftritt: Die mittelalterlichen Alexanderromane mit ihrem spezifischen Motivschatz z.B. leben aus einer spätantiken Tradition. Die Rezeption erfolgt aus einer allgemeinen narrativen Disposition, die dem Abenteuerhaften besonders geneigt ist. In der Geschichte der Wielandfabel ist diese Phase auf niederdeutscher Vorstufe der Thidrekssaga greifbar. Komplexer ist der Aneignungsvorgang, wenn das erzählerische Lehngut in das vorhandene Erzählgut integriert wird – Rezeption als Integration. In diesem Fall knüpft das rezipierte Erzählgut an Eigenes, Vorhandenes an. Ererbte Themen, Inhalte werden dabei fortentwickelt – sei es, daß eine Erzählung eine neue erzählerische Perspektive erhält, sei es, daß stoffmäßiges Wachstum zur epischen Breite führt.

Im Falle des Wielandthemas sind es im wesentlichen zwei Erzählstoffe, die integriert werden: die internationale Wanderfabel von den drei Schwanenmädchen und die spätantiken Künstlerfabeln, zwei auf den ersten Blick ganz disparate Themen mit unterschiedlicher Nähe zur germanischen Schmiedefabel.

Das Erzählgut von den drei Schwanenmädchen,[6] die ihres Gewandes beraubt, eine temporäre Ehe mit menschlichen Wesen eingehen, ist Jan de Vries zufolge attrahiert worden, weil sowohl Wieland als auch diese Schwanenmädchen fliegende Wesen waren. Es wäre nicht mehr als ein „hübscher Gedanke" des Erzählers gewesen, der für diese Rezeption verantwortlich wäre.[7] Dagegen ließe sich anführen: Schwanenmädchenfabel und Rachefabel verbindet ein Gelenk, das in der Volundarkviða tiefere Bedeutung zu haben scheint. Der Ring aus Hervọrs (des Schwanenmädchens) Besitz gelangt zu Bọðvildr, König Níðuðs Tochter, und von ihr wiederum zurück zu Volundr. Volundr erhält damit Gelegenheit, seine Rache zu vollenden und vermutlich auch die Fähigkeit, aus seiner Gefangenschaft zu entfliehen.

Eine Untersuchung von Halldór Halldórsson[8] macht wahrscheinlich, daß es sich bei diesem Ring um einen besonderen Gegenstand handelte, der seiner magischen Fähigkeiten wegen ein notwendiges Requisit in der Fluchtausführung war. Wenn diese Annahme zu recht besteht, läge eine alte Verbindung eines fliegenden weiblichen Wesens mit Wieland vor: Der Ring verklammert

---

[6] H. Holmström, *Studier över svanjungfrumotivet i Volundarkviða och annorstädes.* Malmö 1919.

[7] J. De Vries, „Bemerkungen zur Wielandsage". In: *Edda, Skalden, Saga. FS für Felix Genzmer,* 189.

[8] H. Halldórsson, „Hringtöfrar í íslenzkum orðtökum". In: *Lingua Islandica. Íslenzk Tunga* 2, Reykjavík 1960, 7-31.

Solidus von London: British Museum (Nach Berghaus und Schneider, *Anglo-friesische Runensolidi im Lichte des Neufundes von Schweindorf (Ostfriesland),* Köln, 1967. Tafel I.1).

erzählerisch-strukturell Hervǫr und Wieland in einer Fabelvariante, die uns die Vǫlundarkviða noch erkennen läßt.

Nun gehört der Ring sicherlich nicht zu den strukturellen Merkmalen der Drei-Schwanenmädchen-Fabel. Deren erzählerische Mitte liegt im Raub des Fluggewandes und der zeitweisen Verbindung mit menschlichen Wesen. Wieweit diese bewegende Idee der Wanderfabel zur Rezeption beigetragen hat, muß zunächst noch offen bleiben. Festzuhalten bleibt aber: Ein Ring aus dem Besitz eines fliegenden weiblichen Wesens, das eine temporäre Verbindung mit Wieland eingeht, könnte zum alten Bestand der Schmiedefabel gehört haben. Daraus folgte aber, daß die Schwanenmädchenfabel offensichtlich eine Nähe zur Rachefabel hatte, die nicht nur in dem mehr peripheren Flugvermögen von Schmied und Schwanenjungfrau lag. Die Annahme liegt nahe, daß eine ursprünglichere Wielandfabel bereits eine Verbindung mit einem weiblichen fliegenden Wesen kannte, aus deren Besitz ein Ring stammte, der schließlich Wieland zu Rache und Flucht verhalf. Das Flugvermögen des Schmiedes und der Schwanenmädchen mag also ein Moment im Rezeptions-

Solidus von Harlingen; Leuwarden, Fries Museum (Nach Berghaus und Schneider, Tafel I.2).

vorgang gewesen sein – bedeutsam wurde es aber erst auf einem wesentliche-
ren Hintergrund: einer vermutlich schon bestehenden (zeitweisen) Verbindung Wielands mit einer weiblichen Helferin. Die eddische Vǫlundarkviða
spricht (in der Prosaeinleitung) von Walküren, im Lied selbst von dem *ørlǫg
drýgia*, dem Krieg führen. Wenn das ein Fingerzeig für die ursprüngliche
Natur dieser weiblichen Partnerin des Schmiedes sein dürfte, wäre sie als eine
Art Sieghelferin zu bestimmen.

Als deutliches Lehngut ist noch die Dreizahl der Schwanenmädchen
erkennbar – als Folge dieser 'märchenhaften' Dreizahl werden Vǫlundr dann
wohl auch die Brüder zugeordnet worden sein. So ist es erklärlich, daß in der
Liedfassung, der Vǫlundarkviða, die drei Brüder auf die Schwanenmädchenfabel beschränkt bleiben, nicht aber in die Rachefabel hineinreichen.

Erzählerisches Lehngut wurde auch darin vermutet, daß der exemplarische
Handwerker germanischer Tradition mit den vorbildhaften Künstlern klas-
sischer Überlieferung manche Gemeinsamkeiten aufweist.

Offensichtlich ist die Einwirkung klassischen Erzählgutes auf die Wieland-

fabel in der Version der Thidrekssaga, bzw. bereits ihrer niederdeutschen Vorstufe. Es sind die Erzählungen von Apelles, dem größten Maler des Altertums,
von Daidalos, dem Erfinder und Meister einer archaischen Statuenplastik,
möglicherweise auch von Alexander, dem Bezwinger des Luft- und Wasser-
raumes, die das Wielandthema mitgeformt haben. Die erzählerische Integration dieser Stoffe (Velents Unterwasserfahrzeug, die naturgetreue Statue, die
einen Dieb dingfest machen hilft, der Flugversuch mit Hilfe eines Fluggewandes) ist relativ oberflächlich und verrät 'spielmännischen' Geschmack.

Älter scheint die Integration der Daidalos-Fabel zu sein – genauer gesagt:
das Entweichen aus einer von einem Herrscher erzwungenen Gefangenschaft
mit Hilfe eines Flugapparates. Jan de Vries ging so weit, die Nebenfigur des
Wielandbruders Egill mit Ikaros gleichzusetzen und auch darin klassischen
Einfluß zu vermuten.[9]

So strittig im einzelnen Umfang und Reichweite dieses erzählerischen
Lehngutes auch sein mögen, es ist nicht zu bezweifeln, daß hier antikes
Erzählgut integriert wurde – und das wiederholt. Die jüngere spielmännische
Schicht reichert die Wielandfabel vorwiegend stofflich an, auf älterer Stufe
wird die Fluchtfabel selbst nach klassichem Vorbild gestaltet.

Auch hier ist nach der Ursache solcher Rezeption und Integration zu fragen. Die Forschung rechnet offensichtlich mit einem weitgehend zufälligen
Aufgreifen narrativer Elemente und Themen, die in einem sich weitenden
europäischen Erzählhorizont mehr und mehr zur Verfügung standen. Das
genannte Lehngut läßt aber durchaus einen Zusammenhang und eine Perspektive erkennen. Auf jüngerer Stufe orientiert sich die Rezeption an dem
Gedanken des vorbildhaften Handwerkers und Künstlers, dem nicht nur die
berühmtesten Schwerter und Brünnen zugeschrieben werden, dem vielmehr
auch technische und künstlerische Wunderwerke beigelegt werden. Darin
liegt die Motivation für die Entlehnungsvorgänge dieser Stufe: die Anleihe bei
Apelles, Alexander, Daidalos. Wieland ist nicht nur der Verfertiger der Brün-
ne Beowulfs (Beowulf 455), der Rüstung Walthers (Waldere, Waltharius 965f),
ein berühmter Waffenschmied (Biterolf und Dietleib 156ff), er vertritt für den
heimischen Hörer und Leser auch den klassisch-antiken Künstler: den
Erbauer eines wunderbaren Unterwasserfahrzeuges, den Bildner einer natur-
getreuen Statue, den Erfinder eines luftbeherrschenden Fluggewandes.

Die erste Rezeptionsphase, die mindestens in das 7. Jhd. zurückreicht, folg-

---

[9] J. de Vries, „Bemerkungen zur Wielandsage". In: *Edda, Skalden, Saga. FS für Felix Genzmer*,
187.

te vermutlich bereits einer ähnlichen Erzählstrategie: Der kunstfertige Wieland entkommt aus seiner Gefangenschaft aufgrund seiner Kunstfertigkeit. Wie Daidalos vermag er sich ein Federgewand zu schaffen, das ihm die Flucht ermöglicht. Mitzubedenken ist allerdings auch eine weitere Bezugsmöglichkeit: der soziale Konflikt zwischen einem Herrscher und einem kunstfertigen Gefangenen. Diese Konfliktsituation prägt die antike Fabel ebenso wie die germanische und mag den Rezeptionsvorgang ebenso getragen haben wie das künstlerischhandwerkliche Vermögen der Hauptperson in einer außergewöhnlichen Bedrängnis. Nicht um ein zufälliges Aufgreifen eines antiken Erzählmotives handelte es sich dann, sondern die bewußte Inbezugsetzung zweier exemplarischer Künstler-Handwerker, die ob ihrer polytechnischen Ausnahmequalität verknechtet, letztlich aber gerade dieser Qualität wegen der Gefangenschaft entrinnen.

Im Zusammenhang der antiken Erzählrezeption ist die Frage nicht diskutiert worden, welche Gestalt das unbeeinflußte, rezeptionsfreie germanische Wielandthema gehabt haben könnte.[10] Wohl aber wurde bei der Interpretation eines sehr altertümlichen literarischen Zeugnisses, der Volundarkviða, bemerkt, daß die Fluchtepisode nicht der Federhemd-Variante folgt, sondern das Entkommen aus der Gefangenschaft an den Besitz eines wunderbaren Ringes bindet.

Wenn die Variantenfassungen in eine zeitliche Folge gebracht werden dürfen, bedeutete dies möglicherweise, daß die Ringvariante mit der Rezeption der Daidalos-Fabel durch die Fluggewand-Variante ersetzt wurde. Die im Folgenden versuchte Einbeziehung neuer Bilddenkmäler soll diese These einer ursprünglicheren Wielandfabel erhärten helfen.

Die ikonographischen Quellen

Die ikonographischen Quellen zur Wielandfabel gehören dem 6. bis 8. Jh. an, rücken also in die Nähe der hypothetisch erschlossenen narrativen Frühformen. In der Forschung wurden seit langem das angelsächsische Franks Casket und der gotländische Bildstein von Ardre VIII als Wielanddenkmäler diskutiert. (Vgl. dazu den Bildteil).

Franks Casket, ein Schmuckkästchen mit kostbaren Walbeinschnitzungen,

---

[10] Doch ist immerhin zu vergleichen J. de Vries, „Bemerkungen zur Wielandsage". In: *Edda, Skalden, Saga. FS für Felix Genzmer.*

3

a   b

c

Solidus von Schweindorf; Emden, Ostfriesisches Landesmuseum (Nach Berghaus und Schneider, Tafel II.3).

gehört der Zeit um 700 an.[11] Die Interpretation der uns betreffenden Vorderseite geht von der überzeugenden Beobachtung aus, daß die linke Figur offensichtlich einen Schmied darstellt, der mit der Zange einen menschlichen Kopf über einen Amboß hält und mit der rechten einen Ring, bzw. einen Becher umgreift. Ihm zugewandt ist eine Gestalt mit ausgestrecktem Arm. Der kopflose Torso unter dem Amboß läßt kaum einen Zweifel, daß es sich um die Wielandfabel handelt. Schwieriger sind die Mittelgestalt und die nach rechts gewandte Person zu deuten. Die weibliche Tracht tragende Mittelfigur hält

---

[11] A. Becker, „ Franks Casket. Zu den Bildern und Inschriften des Runenkästchens von Auzon". In: *Sprache und Literatur. Regensburger Arbeiten zur Anglistik und Amerikanistik.* Bd. 5, Hg. v. K.H. Göller. Regensburg 1973.

Brakteat von Dänemark (unbekannter
Fundort); Nationalmuseum Kopenhagen.

einen krugartigen Gegenstand: Die Deutungen reichen von Bǫðvildr, der
Königstochter, bis zu der Magd, die nach der Thidrekssaga den betäubenden
Trank herbeischafft, der Wieland dann erlaubt, seine Rache auszuführen. Als
nicht identifizierte Gestalt kann der Vogelfänger rechts gelten. Doch ist der
Gedanke, es handle sich um den Begleiter Egill, der das Fluggewand
beschafft, nicht von der Hand zu weisen.

Ardre VIII, einer spezifisch gotländischen Quellengattung angehörend, wird
von S. Lindqvist in die 2. Hälfte des 8. Jhs. datiert.[12] Im Gesamtprogramm des
Bildsteines ist auch ein Wielandteil erkennbar: eine Schmiede mit Werk-
zeugen, dahinter die beiden kopflosen Königskinder. Vor der Schmiede Wieland in Vogelgestalt, die abgewandte Person vermutlich Bǫðvildr, die Königstochter.

Im Sinne einer Arbeitshypothese sollen diese Wielanddenkmäler um zwei
weitere Gattungen ikonographischer Quellen vermehrt werden, eine nordsee-
germanische Runensolidigruppe und eine ostseegermanische Brakteatengruppe. (Vgl. dazu den Bilddteil).

---

[12] S. Lindqvist, *Gotlands Bildsteine I-II*. Stockholm 1941-42. L. Buisson, *Der Bildstein Ardre VIII
auf Gotland*. Göttingen 1976. Abh. d. Akad. d. Wiss. Göttingen. Phil.-hist. Kl., 3. Folge Nr. 102.

Ausgangspunkt ist ein 1967 erstmals von P. Berghaus und K. Schneider veröffentlichter ostfriesischer Goldsolidus,[13] gefunden 1948 in Schweindorf, Kreis Wittmund, mit einer runischen Inschrift, **weladu** – einer Inschrift, die nach runischer Orthographie die Möglichkeit bietet, als **welandu** gelesen zu werden. Obwohl diese Lesung bereits von W. Krause und K. Düwel in die Diskussion gebracht wurde,[14] wurde bisher kein Zusammenhang zwischen Bildinhalt und runischer Umschrift hergestellt. Eben dies soll hier versucht werden.

In einer eingehenden numismatisch-ikonographischen Studie stellt P. Berghaus den Schweindorf-Solidus in einen Zusammenhang mit zwei weiteren Runensolidi, den Solidus von Harlingen und einem Solidus aus dem Britischen Museum. Die Gruppe zeigt ikonographisch in der Gestaltung der Rückseite eine rasche Entfernung vom spätantiken Vorbild. Der Solidus von London mutet noch ganz antik an. Der Kaiser hält Labarum und Victoriola mit Kranz. Er tritt auf einen hockenden Gefangenen. Der Harlingen-Solidus zeigt eine Mittelgestalt in einer Art Grube. Ein u-förmiges Seil läuft hinter den Beinen und vor den Armen nach oben offen aus. Eine schwebende Gestalt wendet sich der Mittelfigur zu. Der Schweindorf-Solidus verkürzt die Szene noch mehr: Die Mittelgestalt mit abgewinkelten Armen steht wieder in einer Art Grube. Im Sinne dieser Entfernung vom spätrömischen Vorbild, der Darstellung des Kaiseradventus nämlich, datiert P. Berghaus die drei Solidi: das Londoner Exemplar in das 1. Viertel des 6. Jhs., den Harlinger Solidus in das 3. Viertel, den Schweindorfer Solidus in das 4. Viertel des 6. Jhs.

Alle drei Solidi tragen Runeninschriften, die im Horizont einer frühen Wielandfabel Sinn bekommen könnten. Die Schweindorf-Inschrift **wela(n)du** zeigt ein auslautendes **u**, das bemerkenswert ist. Bereits Krause und Düwel verwiesen in diesem Zusammenhang auf weitere anglofriesische Inschriften auf Knochenkämmen; **kabu, kobu,** die für ein lautgeschichtlich anzusetzendes ***kambaz** stehen. Das bedeutete, daß das auslautende **u** als Reflex der Endungen anglofriesischer **a**-Stämme zu gelten hätte. Die Schweindorf-Inschrift bietet damit – in dieser Interpretation – den ersten Beleg für den Wielandnamen in der Form **Wēlandu** (<***wēlandaz**).

Der London-Solidus trägt die Inschrift **skanomodu.** Sie gilt als die älteste

[13] P. Berghaus, K. Schneider, *Anglo-friesische Runensolidi im Lichte des Neufundes von Schweindorf (Ostfriesland),* Köln und Opladen 1967.

[14] K. Düwel, W.-D. Tempel, „Knochenkämme mit Runeninschriften aus Friesland. Mit einer Zusammenstellung aller bekannten Runenkämme und einem Beitrag zu den friesischen Runeninschriften. Herbert Jankuhn zum 65. Geburtstag". In: *Palaeohistoria,* Vol. XIV, Groningen 1968 (1970), 353-391.

englische Inschrift, wird aber auch für den friesischen Sprachbereich beansprucht. In den bisherigen Deutungen wird darin ein Personenname vermutet, bestehend aus den Namengliedern ***skauno-** (ahd. **Skonhari, Sconrat** usw.) und ***modaz** (ahd. **Baldmuat,** ae. **Modulf** usw.). Das auslautende **u** läßt sich auch hier in analoger Weise zu **Welandu** als Reflex der **az**-Endung erklären. Nicht zwingend ist dagegen der Ansatz eines Personennamens. Denkbar ist auch ein Appellativum, gebildet mit dem Grundwort ***modaz,** das gerade im heroischen Kontext gut verankert ist (ae. **mōd,** an. **móðr**). Wenn **skano** mit „schön" zu verbinden ist (ae. **scïene, scëne** beautiful, bright, brilliant, light), bedeutete dies eine positive Qualifikation des **modu.** Auch als Apellativ ließe sich ein solches Kompositum in Verbindung mit einem heroischen Bildinhalt begreifen („strahlender Mut" oder dergleichen).

Die Inschrift des Harlinger Solidus lautet **hada.** Auch hier wurde zunächst an einen Personennamen, d.h. die Kurzform eines Namens mit ***hadu-** Kampf gedacht. Auch hier ist jedoch die appellativische Möglichkeit zu bedenken. Wenn im auslautenden **u** ein Endungsreflex vermutet werden darf, gälte Gleiches für das **a** in **hada.** Eine lautliche Entsprechung zu **hada** böte dann altenglisch **heador** n. (restraint, confinement, receptaculum) oder altenglisch **headu-** (Kampf- ae. nur in Komposita belegt).

Lassen sich diese Inschriften nun sinnvoll auf den Bildinhalt beziehen? Dazu ist zunächst auf die Fabelvariante in Deors Klage zu verweisen, wo von Wēlund gesagt wird, er habe **be wurman** „ bei den Schlangen", d.h. offensichtlich in einer Schlangengrube, Elend erfahren, Nidhad habe ihn in Fesseln gelegt (**on nede legde**).[15]

Die Vermutung liegt nahe, daß der Schweindorf-Solidus diese zwanghafte Behausung wiedergibt: eine grubenartige Einfassung, in der die berockte Gestalt steht. Auch der Harlingen-Solidus hat Anzeichen einer solchen Einfassung. Ist die Inschrift **hada** im Sinne receptaculum darauf zu beziehen? Charakteristisch für Harlingen ist ein Band, das hinter den Beinen und vor den Armen der Mittelgestalt nach oben ausläuft. Auf späteren Runensteinen ist die bandartige Umschlingung menschlicher Gestalten ähnlich hinter und vor den Gliedmaßen geführt. Sollte damit die Fesselung der Mittelgestalt ausgedrückt werden? Der London-Solidus steht dem spätantiken Vorbild noch so nahe, daß kaum entschieden werden kann, ob hier bereits eine germanische Interpretation vorliegt. Erst die Harlingen- und Schweindorf-Solidi machen

---

[15] „Deors Klage". In: *The Anglo-Saxon Poetic Records.* A Collective Edition. III. The Exeter Book, hg. v. G. P. Krapp. New York/London 1936, 178-179.

klar, daß die Rezeption in Richtung Wieland verläuft. Auf diesem Wege wurde die kranzführende Victoria in der Harlingen-Fassung augenscheinlich als wesentlicher Bestandteil angesehen. Die Schweindorf-Fassung verkürzt die Darstellung so weit, daß nur noch Welandu in der Grube übrig bleibt.

Die Arbeitshypothese besteht also im Blick auf die nordseegermanischen Runensolidi darin, daß zunächst die Runeninschriften auf die bildlichen Darstellungen bezogen werden und daß weiterhin diese Inschriften im Horizont einer frühen Wielandfabel gelesen werden: Wieland (Schweindorf) – Gefängnis (Harlingen) (Unentschieden bleibt die Zuordnung der **skanomodo**-Inschrift auf dem London-Solidus).

Aus der Verbindung von Runeninschrift und Bilddarstellung ergibt sich die Lesung: Wieland in seinem Gefängnis (Schweindorf), ein übernatürliches weibliches Wesen – als Entsprechung der spätrömischen Victoria – ihm zugewandt (Harlingen).

Es wirkt suggestiv, die ikonographischen Fixierungen Wielands in seiner tiefsten Erniedrigung zusammen zu sehen mit der erzählerischen Strategie eines Deor-Dichters: der Vertiefung nämlich in die Unglückssituation von Gestalten der Heldensage (Wieland in der Grube, Beadohild in erzwungener Mutterschaft, die Krieger unter Eormanrics tyrannischer Herrschaft usw.). Die augenblickliche schlimme Lage weckt aber auch die Hoffnung auf eine bessere Zukunft. Selbst die Inschriften und Bilder des Franks Casket scheinen nach einem solchen Plan angeordnet zu sein: Die Inschriften nennen ja auch solche Extremsituationen, den aus seinem Lebenselement geworfenen Fisch, ein unbekanntes Wesen auf einem Unheilsberge, Romulus und Remus der Heimat fern, Jerusalems Einwohner auf der Flucht. Es wäre dann folgerichtig, daß gerade in einer nordseegermanischen Denkmälergruppe zur Wielandfabel ein elegischer Zug greifbar würde – ein Zug, der so weit gehen könnte, daß, wie auf Schweindorf, nur noch der Held in seiner zwanghaften Behausung sichtbar wäre.

Wenn die spätrömische Darstellung des Kaiseradventus in dieser nordseegermanischen Solidigruppe als Wielandfabel rezipiert wurde, dann wäre es folgerichtig, auch die ostseegermanischen Brakteaten, die vom gleichen Thema des Kaiseradvents abhängen, auf ihre germanische Interpretation hin zu befragen. Zu dieser Ostseegruppe gehören insgesamt sieben B-Brakteaten, die mit einer Ausnahme alle aus dem dänischen Bereich stammen. Mackeprang[16] und

---

[16] M. B. Mackeprang, „De nordiske Guldbrakteater". In: *Jysk Arkæologisk Selskabs Skrifter*, Bd. II, Aarhus 1952.

Öberg[17] sind sich in ihren Brakteatenuntersuchungen einig, daß das ikonographische Vorbild dieser Brakteaten in den Revers-Darstellungen römischer Goldmünzen zu suchen ist, die den Kaiseradvent beinhalten. Zu datieren sind diese Brakteaten in die 1. Hälfte des 7. Jhs.

Eigentümlich ist für diese dänischen Brakteaten eine weitgehende Stilisierung und Typisierung des Dargestellten: Einer maßstablich überhöhten Mittelfigur ist immer eine Nachfolgegestalt mit abwärts weisendem Speer und eine entgegenblickende weibliche geflügelte Gestalt zugeordnet. Die Mittelgestalt bewegt sich innerhalb einer rechtwinkligen Einfassung. Ein in Schrittstellung befindliches Bein ist hoch angezogen, der Oberschenkel des Standbeines merkwürdig verdickt.

Wollte man die literarische Überlieferung auf diese ostseegermanischen Brakteaten anwenden, so wäre in der Mittelgestalt Wieland zu sehen, dem sich ein übermenschliches weibliches Wesen mit einem heilbringenden Ring zuwendet. Die nachfolgende Gestalt wäre nach narrativer Tradition entweder König Níðuðr, von dem es in der Vǫlundarkviða heißt, daß niemand außer ihm es wagte, Wieland in seiner Behausung aufzusuchen, oder Egill, der Meisterschütze. Wenn Egill erst unter dem Einfluß der Daidalossage attrahiert wurde, schiede diese Möglichkeit aus. Ein immer nach unten weisender Speer signalisierte dann möglicherweise die kriegerische Ohnmacht angesichts des wunderbaren Geschehens, dessen Zeuge er ist.

Charakteristische ikonographische Züge sind insbesondere der Mittelgestalt eigen, die wir in Verfolgung dieser Hypothese mit Wieland identifizieren. Was bedeuten die angewinkelten, nach oben und unten weisenden Arme mit den seltsamen „technischen" Fortsetzungen? Sollte es eine Wieland-Chiffre sein? Was bedeuten die gekreuzten Beine, die auf den Brakteaten dieser Gruppe die Mittelgestalt charakterisieren? Es scheint die Stilisierung eines 'Hahnenschrittes' vorzuliegen, bei dem durch pathologische Veränderungen am Bein der Fuß höher als normal angehoben werden muß, um nicht am Boden zu schleifen. Es wäre eine glückliche Erfassung eines charakteristischen Bewegungsablaufes bei einer pathologischen Deformation des Beines, die der Brakteatenkünstler hier anschaulich macht.[18] Wenn hier die ikonographische Stili-

---

[17] H. Öberg, „Guldbrakteaterna från Nordens folkvandringstid". In: *Kungl. Vitterhets Historie och Antikvitets Akademiens Handlingar,* Del 53, Stockholm 1942.

[18] Den Herren Kollegen Prof. Dr. K. Dieckhöfer und Prof. Dr. N. Mani von der medizinischen Fakultät der Rheinischen Friedrich-Wilhelms-Universität Bonn habe ich in diesem Zusammenhang herzlich zu danken. Auf ihr Urteil stützt sich die Annahme, daß die ikonographisch auffällige Beinhaltung einen „Hahnenschritt" (auch „Steppergang" genannt) wiedergeben könnte.

Brakteat von Skovsborg;
Nationalmuseum Kopenhagen.

sierung als Veranschaulichung einer Beinlähmung zu verstehen ist, bedeutete dies für die Interpretation einen glücklichen Umstand, denn die Lähmung ist ein charakteristisches und individuelles Kennzeichen der Wielandfigur. Eine beachtliche Detailvariation liegt darin, daß in der Beresinaversion[19] die Mittelgestalt selbst den Ring führt, die weibliche Gestalt einen Zweig. Der Zweig stammt aus der spätrömischen Vorlage und ist dort ein Sieg- und Friedenszeichen. Wenn in der germanischen Rezeption Zweig und Ring zwischen weiblicher Gestalt und Mittelgestalt wechseln, ließe sich das im Rahmen der Wieland-Interpretation begreifen.

Der erst kürzlich gefundene Gummerup-Brakteat[20] bestätigt die Version von Skovsborg, in der ein schlangenartiges Wesen an der Ferse der Mittelgestalt angreift, wandelt aber die Ausrüstung der weiblichen Gestalt so ab, daß in der einen Hand der Ring, in der anderen das Schwert geführt wird – ein unmiß-

[19] M. B. Mackeprang, „De Nordiske Guldbrakteater". In: *Jysk Arkæologisk Selskabs Skrifter,* Bd. II, Aarhus 1952, Pl. 6, Nr. 16.

[20] Abgebildet und beschrieben bei K. Hauck, „Zur Ikonologie der Goldbrakteaten, V: Ein neues Drei-Götter-Amulett von der Insel Fünen". In: *Geschichte in der Gesellschaft. FS für Karl Bosl zum 65. Geburtstag,* hg. v. F. Prinz. u.a., Stuttgart 1974, 92-159. Auf K. Haucks ganz andere Deutung, die hier nicht aufgenommen werden kann, sei hier verwiesen.

Brakteat von Faxe;
Nationalmuseum Kopenhagen.

verständlicher Hinweis auf den kriegerischen Charakter dieser übernatürlichen Person. Dabei ist zu erinnern, daß noch in der Vǫlundarkvïða das **ǫrlog**
drýgja = Krieg führen zum Geschäft der 3 Schwanenmädchen gehört – im seltsamen Widerspruch zum Wesen der 3 Schwanenmädchen im internationalen
Erzählgut. Ikonographisch ist die Schlangenversion von spätrömischen Vor-
bildern abhängig, in denen der Herrscher eine Schlange niedertritt. Die Brakteaten stilisieren um und zeigen die Schlange als angreifendes Wesen. Die
interpretatorische Frage lautete, ob hier Deors Klage, derzufolge Wēlund **be**
wurman Not litt, aufschlußreich sein könnte.

Die Tücke der Überlieferung will es, daß eine sinngebende Runeninschrift
der B-Brakteatengruppe möglicherweise auf dem Killerup-Brakteat vorgelegen hatte. Das erhaltene Fragment läßt eindeutig die Zugehörigkeit zu dieser dänischen Gruppe erkennen; die noch erkennbare Inschrift endet auf
-undR. Es bleibt nicht mehr als eine Möglichkeit, in Analogie zum Schweindorfsolidus auch hier eine Vǫlundr-Inschrift zu vermuten.[21]
Die ikonographische Gestalt der Solidi- und Brakteatengruppe läßt deutlich
die Abhängigkeit von spätrömischen Vorlagen erkennen, andererseits aber
auch die Neuinterpretation unverkennbar erscheinen. Hier muß ein hei-

[21] L. Jacobsen, E. Moltke, *Danmarks Runeindskrifter,* Kopenhagen 1942, Sp. 517-518.

misches Erzählthema vorgelegen haben, in dessen Dienst die bildliche Vorlage gestellt wurde – das gälte ganz unabhängig von der Tatsache, ob man nun eine solche Wielandinterpretation akzeptiert oder nicht. Der Schweindorfsolidus mit seiner **Welandu-** Inschrift spricht für eine solche Interpretation der Nordseegruppe. Die dänischen Brakteaten müßten nicht notwendigerweise gleichen Bedeutungsgehalt haben. Doch lassen die angeführten Indizien es ratsam erscheinen, auch diese Möglichkeit zu bedenken.

Die jüngeren Bilddenkmäler zum Wielandthema, d.h. Franks Casket und Ardre VIII, zeigen einige bedeutsame Übereinstimmungen, die sie von der älteren Kleinkunst abheben. Zunächst ist ein komplexerer Aufbau des Wielandthemas im Vergleich mit Brakteaten und Solidi bemerkenswert.

Inhaltlich setzen sie einen entscheidenden Entwicklungsschritt des Wielandthemas voraus: An die Stelle des Ringes, der Wieland die Flucht aus seinem Gefängnis ermöglicht, ist eine Fluggewandung getreten – signalisiert durch die vogelfangende Gestalt des Walbeinkästchens und die Vogelgestalt vor der Schmiede auf dem Bildstein. Damit verbunden ist das Zurücktreten der geflügelten weiblichen Helferin – an ihre Stelle tritt eine andere Frauengestalt, Bǫðvildr, die geschändete Königstochter. Das Thema erhält damit eine schwerpunktmäßige Verlagerung: Wohl stimmten ältere und jüngere Bilddenkmäler darin überein, daß sie den dramatischen Verlauf in dem Moment fixieren, da für Wieland die Flucht aus dem Gefängnis realisierbar erscheint – Franks Casket und Ardre VIII tun dies aber unter Einbeziehung einer vorangehenden Rache an den Königskindern. Davon zeugen die kopflosen Körper hinter der Schmiede, die sich entfernende Frauengestalt vor der Schmiede auf Ardre VIII, der Rumpf unter dem Amboß, der Kopf in der Schmiedezange und die Frauengestalt vor Wieland auf Franks Casket.

Der Schwerpunkt verschiebt sich damit von einer Fluchtfabel, Fluchthilfe eines übermenschlichen Wesens, zu einer Rachefabel, grausame Rache eines Schmiedes und anschließendes Entkommen mit Hilfe eines Fluggewandes.

Wie im einzelnen die Rache Wielands in der Fabel der Solidi-Stufe aussah, wissen wir nicht – sie kann durchaus schon die Gestalt der erzählenden Bilddenkmäler des 8. Jahrhunderts gehabt haben.

Die neue Entwicklungsstufe bestand offensichtlich in der Einführung einer neuen, rationalistischeren Fluchtvariante – und dies wohl unter dem Einfluß der klassischen Daidalos-Sage. Wenn Franks Casket als das früheste Denkmal, das diese Version zeigt, einen Fingerzeig über Ort und Zeit dieser Neuerung herzugeben vermag, dann wäre an England um 700 als Ort und Zeit dieser Rezeption zu denken.

Die These lautet also zusammenfassend gesagt: Eine germanische Fabel von einem kunstfertigen Schmied, der von einem Herrscher gewaltsam, d.h. unter Lähmung seiner Gliedmaßen, in Dienst gezwungen wurde, befreit sich nach grausamer Rache mit Hilfe eines übermenschlichen fliegenden weiblichen Wesens aus seinem Gefängnis.

Um 700 erfuhr dieses Thema unter dem Einfluß spätantiker Sagenüberlieferung vom kunstfertigen Daidalos und Ikaros eine Umwandlung, die die magische Flucht mittels eines Ringes ersetzte durch die rationalistischere Variante einer Flucht mit Hilfe eines Federkleides. Möglicherweise ist an die Stelle der Fluchthelferin ein Fluchthelfer getreten, der dann mit Egill identifiziert wurde.

Zum Verhältnis von Bild- und Wortdenkmälern im Umkreis des Wielandthemas

Wenn eine Dimension narrativer Technik die zeitliche Abfolge des Erzählten, die Erzählzeit ist, so ist die entsprechende Dimension ikonographischer Technik der visuelle (2- oder 3dimensionale) Raum, der Erzählraum. Zeit und Raum sind jedoch nur die Vorgegebenheiten, die erst in dem Augenblick zu artistischen Gestaltungsmitteln wurden, da der Künstler sie in ein ganz bestimmtes Verhältnis zum Erzählgeschehen in seiner natürlichen Raum-Zeit-Dimension setzt.

Die Vǫlundarkviða erreicht in ihrer letzten Szene, Wielands Fluchtoffenbarung vor dem König, eine fast 100-%ige Deckung von Erzählzeit und erzählter Zeit, d.h. die Erzählung verläuft fast ausschließlich in direkter Rede. Im Blick auf den völlig dialogfreien ersten Teil des Liedes, der Schwanenmädchengeschichte, ergibt sich ein deutliches Gefälle hin zu der Szene, da Wieland im Begriffe ist, sich aus seinem Gefängnis zu erheben und König und Königin die furchtbare Rache offenbart.

Die narrative Rachefabel besteht nicht darin, das grausame Rachegeschehen an den unschuldigen Opfern auszugestalten (der Erzähler berichtet hier nur knapp), sondern in der Demütigung des Herrscherpaares, im Triumph des entfliehenden Schmiedes.

Der Bildkünstler muß auf ganz andere Weise mit seinen Vorgegebenheiten fertig werden, um die Relation seines Erzählraumes zum Erzählgeschehen künstlerisch fruchtbar zu machen. Auf den Brakteaten können wir eine sehr archaische Problembewältigung beobachten: Der Künstler bedient sich bei seinen Figuren eines unterschiedlichen Maßstabes. Die Mittelgestalt erscheint

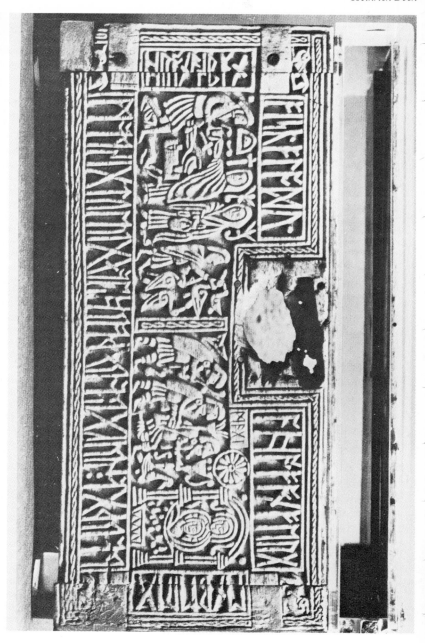

überproportional groß, die Frauen- und begleitende Männergestalt immer kleiner. Solche Beobachtungen machen wir auch bei vendelzeitlichen Bilddenkmälern und weiteren frühmittelalterlichen Darstellungen. Damit ist kein natürlicher Maßstab gemeint, sondern ein künstlerischer. Es ist ein Mittel des Darstellers, innerhalb seiner Raumvorgabe eine Bedeutungsdifferenzierung, eine Zu- und Nebenordnung, mit anderen Worten eine gewisse Erzählperspektive darzutun. Offensichtlich weist dieser Bedeutungsmaßstab auf die Mittelfigur, die wir hypothetisch als Wieland bezeichnet haben. Von ihm her ist die Darstellung zu lesen – er ist das Subjekt der Aussage, seine Geschichte ist es, nicht die des weiblichen Wesens, nicht die der Folgegestalt. Das ist nicht unwichtig – gerade auch in der Lesung der oft schwer deutbaren Signa auf Brakteaten. Als eine methodische Möglichkeit läßt sich daraus der Schluß ziehen: Wenn es gelingt, die erzählerische Perspektive eines Denkmals festzulegen, erhalten auch so 'unbesetzte' Zeichen wie Kreuze, Wedel, Dreiecke etc. eine Gerichtetheit, sind als Attribuiertes der Bedeutungsrichtung eines Denkmals zuzuordnen.

Zur korrekten Erfassung der Erzählperspektive setzt der Künstler noch ein weiteres ikonographisches Mittel ein: das geschriebene Wort in Gestalt von In-, Um- oder Unterschriften. Die Funktion solcher ikonographischen Elemente besteht darin, die von einem Bild geweckten Konnotationen in die rechte Bahn zu lenken – den in der Grube Stehenden eben als Wieland zu identifizieren, mit **skanomodu** den Triumph des Helden über seinen Gegner anzudeuten. Selbst das künstlerisch hochstehende Walbeinkästchen arbeitet mit dieser Technik. Die Magierszene wird durch eine Inschrift **Magi** in ihrer Bedeutung festgelegt, eine Egilszene durch eine Inschrift **Egli**. Diese Einbeziehung des schriftlichen Wortes scheint eine ebenso archaische wie moderne Technik zu sein: ein Versuch, die Konnotationen in die beabsichtigte Richtung zu lenken.

Das Problem der Konnotation scheint überhaupt ein elementares Interpretationsanliegen zu sein. Denn nur dann, wenn wir mit den ikonographischen Elementen die rechte Konnotation verbinden, vermögen wir auch zur Bildbedeutung vorzudringen. Unser Verstehensdefizit wird dabei besonders deutlich, wenn wir Zeichen, Tierbilder, Gesten usw. zwar in ihrer Vordergründigkeit erkennen, ihren Sinn aber nicht verstehen. Ein bezeichnendes Beispiel sind die Gebärden, die in frühmittelalterlicher germanischer Kunst überaus häufigen ausdrucksstarken Arm-, Bein- und Körperhaltungen. Zweifellos haben all diese spezifischen Gebärden ihren ganz bestimmten konnotativen Sinn: die verrenkten Beine, die abgewinkelten Arme, die verdrehten Körper. Da wir

Bildstein Ardre VIII (Nach Buisson).

ganz aus dieser Tradition gefallen sind, verstehen wir den Sinn dieser Gebärden nicht mehr – die adäquate Konnotation stellt sich nicht ein.

Anders als die Brakteaten verfahren die jüngeren Denkmäler, Franks Casket und Bildstein. Was der Bedeutungsmaßstab auf den Brakteaten leistet, bietet hier eine szenische Konsequenz, d.h. in der Abfolge von Einzeldarstellungen manifestiert sich eine Geschehensrichtung und damit auch eine Erzählperspektive. Franks Casket dürften wir so lesen: Die Rache des Schmiedes glückt – unter dem Amboß liegt bereits ein Knabentorso, die Königstochter ist in der Schmiede; die Fluchtvorbereitung, d.h. der Fang der Vögel, ist im Gange. Das ist offensichtlich die Erzählperspektive: aus der Erniedrigung zur Befreiung!

Diese Lesung von links nach rechts entspricht in etwa der des Bildsteines in gegenläufiger Szenenfolge: rechts die Schmiede mit den kopflosen Knaben, links anschließend der mit dem Vogelgewand entfliehende Wieland, die Königstochter den Ort verlassend. Die räumliche Konkretisierung des Zeitfaktors mittels szenischer Reihung bringt die Erzählperspektive des Künstlers zum Ausdruck: Nach der Rache an den Königskindern flieht Wieland mit einem Fluggewand. Franks Casket und Bildstein stimmen darin überein, daß in dieser Perspektive der königliche Gegenpart keinen Platz hat. Im Rache-Flucht-Zusammenhang tauchen allein Wieland, die Knaben und Bodvildr auf. Das bedeutet eine nicht unerhebliche Verschiebung der Thematik von der mirakulösen Lösung des Herrscher-Gefangenen-Konfliktes hin zu der rationalistischeren, privateren Rachefabel der jüngeren Stufe. Die geschichtliche Entwicklung des Wielandthemas beginnt für uns erkennbar im 6. Jh. – d.h. in einer Zeit, da unter dem Einfluß spätrömischer Bildgestaltung auch im germanischen Norden das Bild neben das Wort trat. Die formale Abhängigkeit ist zunächst deutlich erkennbar. Die inhaltliche Uminterpretation des Kaiseradventus zur Wielandfabel, durch eine Umschrift gesichert, setzt offensichtlich an der Sieghilfe eines übernatürlichen weiblichen Wesens an. Ein Ring fungiert dabei als symbolisches, bzw. magisch-dingliches Zeichen. Diese frühe Version ist für uns nicht mehr weiter durchdringbar.[22]

---

[22] Weiter führen allenfalls Überlegungen, wie sie zuletzt A. Mozsolics, „Hephaistos Sántasága". In: *Communicationes de Historia Artis Medicinae,* Budapest, angestellt hat. Aus der Tatsache, daß in Sage und Mythos Schmiede oft lahm sind oder hinken, schließt er, daß man die Lähmung als Arbeitsschädigung auffassen kann, die durch das Einwirken von Arsengasen verursacht sei. Darin läge dann das ursprünglichste Substrat der Mythenbildung. Den Hinweis verdanke ich der Freundlichkeit von Elisabeth Vestergaard, Etnografisk Afd., Moesgård, Aarhus Universitet.

Ausschnitt: Bildstein Ardre VIII (mit Wielandszene) (Nach Buisson).

Die Metamorphose der Fabel erreicht eine neue Stufe, als der exemplarische Künstler und Handwerker antiker Prägung von Wieland beansprucht wird. Die Fluchtfabel erhielt damit eine rationalere Gestaltung. Das Federgewand ermöglicht nun das Entweichen. Gleichzeitig wurde damit die Verbindung zu der übernatürlichen Fluchthelferin gelockert. Die Folge zeigt sich in der Ab- und Umwandlung dieses Sagenzuges durch das Wandergut von den drei Schwanenmädchen. Als Kernfabel, ererbt und durch alle Wandlungen hindruch bewahrt, erweist sich die grausame Rache des in Frondienst gezwungenen Handwerkers. Um diesen Kern lagert sich beweglicheres Erzählgut als deutlicher Indikator geschichtlichen Wandels.

Rheinische Friedrich-Wilhelms-Universität Bonn

Some pictorial conventions for the recounting of thoughts and experiences in late medieval art

by Sixten Ringbom

The influence of literature on the visual arts was probably more powerful and more direct during the middle ages than at any other stage of European civilization, the Renaissance not excepted. Not only did medieval art rely upon texts and traditions for its subject matter. Even the rules and conventions for pictorial representation seem to have been affected by the examples set by literature. This influence is especially felt in the technique of pictorial narration, a technique that during the middle ages was developed to fit literary requirements rather than the possibilities and limitations of graphic representation.

The predominance of the word over the image in Christian art is, of course, easy to explain. The canonical books of the Bible contain a wealth of narrative works. Apocrypha, pseudepigrapha and legendary texts of various kinds added to the corpus of narrative material for which artists were expected to find or invent visual equivalents. The subservience of pictorial art was even laid down in the theology of art: religious painting was to the illiterate what the Scripture was to those who were able to read: Nam quod legentibus scriptura, hoc idiotis praestat pictura cernentibus (St. Gregory, *Letters,* 11:13).

Ever since the early Christian period artists were faced with the problem of translating verbal accounts into visual terms, frequently, as in book art, in close connexion with the text to be illustrated. From a modest beginning in late classical illustration of epic poetry and Septuagint texts book illumination rose to the position of a major art. This development was highly important for the emergence of pictorial narrative and from then on "the *art of storytelling in pictures* became inextricably linked with the history of book-illumination".[1]

---

[1] See Kurt Weitzmann's contribution to the symposium on Narration in Ancient Art (1955): "Narration in Early Christendom" *(Am. Journ. of Archaeol.,* 61, 1957, pp. 83-91), p. 83. Also Meyer Schapiro, *Words and Pictures, On the Literal and the Symbolic in the Illustration of a Text,* The Hague 1973 *(Approaches to Semiotics, paperback Series,* 11).

Narrative devices (Direct Narration)

1. Cyclic narrative

I.

II.

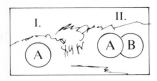

 = protagonists of story

I, II = phases of story

hence: I-II represents temporal flow

2. Continuous narrative

Devices for depicting the content of speech, dreams, visions, thoughts etc. (Indirect Narration)

3. *Contiguity* of scenes of a cycle

I. II. I. II.

 or

 = speaker, dreamer, thinker, author etc.

X = content of speech, dream, vision, thought, text etc.

4. *Juxtaposition* of speaker etc. and content

 or

(where $\textcircled{A}$ is qualified with attributes and paraphernalia suggesting X)

5. *Differentiation* of levels

6. *Appendage* of subordinate motif

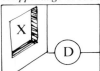

Fig. 1. Joseph dreaming about the sheaves; Joseph telling his brothers about his dream. Vienna Genesis, Österreichische Nationalbibliothek, Cod.theol. graec.31, p.28 (Photo Bildarchiv d.Öst. Nationalbibl.). In this cyclical narrative the identity of Joseph in the two scenes is established by means of physiognomical features. The content of the dream is expressed through the juxtaposition of Joseph and the sheaves, and the content of the speech through the contiguity of the dream scene and the conversation scene.

To the painter the text presented both a challenge and a support. The challenge lay in the difficulty of representing events that are easily recounted in words but hard to depict in an image. The support offered by the text was as useful as it is obvious. A book illustration does not have to be self-explanatory; a reader follows the text and the images more or less simultaneously, the image presenting a gloss to the text and the text a caption to the image. In other fields of art, too, captions may help the beholder to grasp what the picture is about. Repeated use of the same iconographic formula may also make literary themes easily recognizable.

One challenge, which the illustrator of a narrative has to face, is the rendering of the *temporal* flow in which the events follow one after another. Ancient art devised two solutions to this problem: picture cycles and continuous narration. Both methods presuppose certain conventions, such as the identity of the person A in scene I with the person A in scene II etc. This identity is normally established by means of physiognomical detail and particularities of dress, attributes and the like. Both the cyclical and the continuous method were adopted by early Christian illuminators, a development which has been analyzed with admirable lucidity by Kurt Weitzmann.[2]

One thing, however, is to depict the overt action of a story, that is, what the persons are doing – quite another matter is to find visual equivalents to what they are saying, thinking, assuming, perceiving, dreaming etc. In a verbal context talk, thoughts, dreams etc. are so easy to recount by indirect speech that we rarely think of it as a problem. We may indicate what linguists like to call 'the proposition of content' by means of suitable verbs ('say', 'think', 'dream' etc.), grammatical construction ('that'-clauses, subjunctive mood), punctuation (colon, quotation marks) or a combination of these. But what should a painter do? What means are there to the painter's disposal for expressing what the protagonists of his picture say, think, believe, see or dream?

In his book on *The Rise of Pictorial Narrative in Twelfth-Century England* Otto Pächt has discussed a solution to the problem, a solution already known to late classical art (Fig. 1) and again used by twelfth-century English illuminators in the St. Albans Psalter. For the sake of convenience we shall here refer to this expedient as *contiguity* of the scenes of a picture cycle. The St. Albans master has thus overcome a difficulty that a German copy of the English composition simply evaded by introducing text scrolls containing the conversation between

[2] Cf. note (1), and Weitzmann, *Illustrations in Roll and Codex, A Study of the Origin and Method of Text Illustration*, Princeton 1947.

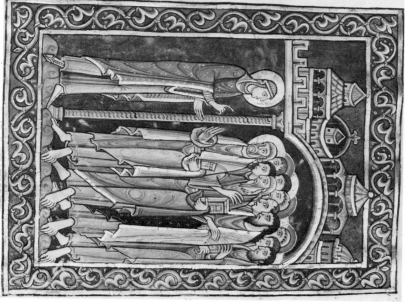

Figs. 2-3. The three Maries at the sepuchre; Mary Magdalen addressing the disciples. St. Albans Psalter, Holdesheim, St. Gotthard, pp. 50-51 (Photo The Warburg Institute Photographic Collection).

Mary Magdalen and the Disciples after Resurrection. Instead of resorting to text scrolls the St. Albans master placed the scene of the *Three Maries at the Sepulchre* on the lefthand page and the scene of *Mary Magdalen Addressing the Disciples* on the righthand page. Hence the opening of the book becomes a whole, suggesting what exactly Mary Magdalen is telling the disciples. (Figs. 2-3).[3]

Contiguity may also be used for suggesting what a person in a picture says or thinks about future events; that is for prophecies, prophetical dreams etc. But this versatility also introduces an element of ambiguity (except, perhaps, in the case of a book opening where the two facing pages are presented as a pair). Attempts to remove this ambiguity can be observed in thirteenth-century cyclic illustration. The *Bible moralisée* manuscripts contain a wealth of ingenious pictorial devices contrived to give precision to the narrative. The moralized Bible reintegrated by Alexandre de Laborde from elements in the Bibliothèque Nationale, The British Library and the Bodleian Library is particularly remarkable in this respect.[4] Let us compare two narrative representations from this early fourteenth-century manuscript.

Fig. 4 shows a leaf with scenes from the infancy of Christ according to Matth. 2:11-13,15. In the third medallion on the left an angel appears to the Magi in a dream; we learn from the caption that the angel tells the kings not to return to Herod, as they had been invited to do. In the top roundel on the right the Magi have indeed returned home by a different route. The content of the angel's message is suggested by the contiguity of the two scenes (the intervening roundel is a moralization not belonging to the narrative).

A different method of accounting for the content of a dream is employed in the third medallion on the right, where the angel instructs St. Joseph to flee to Egypt with the holy family. This scene can be interpreted as a continuous narrative consisting of two distinct events, the nightly appearance of the angel and the journey to Egypt. The content of the angel's message has been made clear enough – but to a price. For without knowing what the whole story is about or reading the caption there is no way of telling that the miniature represents St. Joseph's dream, or, indeed, that it represents a dream at all.

The method employed in the latter example may be termed *juxtaposition.*

---

[3] Otto Pächt, *The Rise of Pictorial Narrative in Twelfth-Century England,* Oxford 1962, p. 46f. Cf. Otto Pächt, C. R. Dodwell & Francis Wormald, *The St. Albans Psalter (Albani Psalter),* London 1960 (*Studies of the Warburg Institute, 25*).

[4] Alexandre de Laborde (ed.), *La Bible moralisée illustrée conservée à Oxford, Paris et Londres,* 1-5, Paris 1911-1927.

Fig. 4. Scenes from the childhood of Jesus with moralizations. Bible moralisée, The British Library, MS. Harley 1527, fol. 12v (Photo The British Library).

Juxtaposition is related to contiguity in roughly the same way as continuous narrative is related to cyclic. Like the continuous method juxtaposition can be traced back to late classical and early Christian illumination. It occurs in the Vatican Virgil,[5] and it is successfully exploited in the Vienna Genesis for the depicting of Abraham's, Joseph's and Pharaoh's dreams.[6]

Among Old Testament themes the story of Joseph and his brethren is of particular interest since it introduces yet another level of narration: Joseph tells his family *that* he had dreamt *that* the sheaves and the stars made obeisance to him. Ever since the Vienna Genesis these subordinate that-clauses were translated into visual terms by a combination of contiguity and juxtaposition. The sleeping figure of Joseph is juxtaposed, first, with the sheaves (Fig. 1) and, second, with the sun, moon and the eleven stars. The dream representations then form parts of a cycle where they are followed by scenes showing Joseph expounding his dreams to his brothers and parents.

By repeated use, juxtaposition becomes a conventional device for dream scenes where a standardized figure, the reclining dreamer, becomes a kind of pictorial quotation mark, an index telling the beholder that the picture deals with a dream. The device is used as a matter of course for dream themes ranging from the lives of the saints to secular romance. Indeed, it looks as if the mere presence of a reclining figure invited the medieval beholder to interpret any scene containing this figure as a dream, including scenes that had nothing at all to do with dreaming. This is apparently what happened at some early stage of the iconography of the Tree of Jesse (Fig. 5). This motif, we recall, is a pictorial translation of Isaiah's prophecy about the stem which was to grow forth from the root of Isai, King David's father. As such this allegory contains no dream element whatever. Early representations of the theme show Jesse sitting with the tree in his lap, or, in another version, resting in a sarcophagus with the tree trunk passing through his dead body. Usually Jesse is represented as simply reclining with closed eyes. It was this last type of image that, by analogy with the iconographies of the sleeping Adam and Jacob's dream, became understood as a dream. The reclining figure was taken as the dreamer and the tree as the dream.[7]

[5] J. De Wit, *Die Miniaturen des Vergilius Vaticanus,* Amsterdam 1959, pl. 9.

[6] Paul Buberl, *Die byzantinischen Handschriften,* 1: *Der Wiener Dioskurides und Die Wiener Genesis,* Leipzig 1937 (*Die illuminierten Handschriften und Inkunabeln der Nationalbibliothek in Wien,* IV), figs. 28, 29, 35.

[7] Gertrud Schiller, *Ikonographie der christlichen Kunst,* Bd 1, 1966, p. 28; A. Thomas, "Wurzel Jesse", in: *Lexikon der christlichen Ikonographie,* Rome & Freiburg 1972, Bd IV, col. 551.

Fig. 5. The Tree of Jesse. Stained glass, Abbey Church of Saint-Denis, *detail* (Photo Service Photographique).

Fig. 6. The dreamer in bed. Roman de la Rose, Bibliothèque Nationale, Ms.fr. 1564, fol. 1r (Photo Bibl. Nat.).

Fig. 7. The monk's vision. Gautier de Coincy, Miracles de Nostre Dame, Leningrad, Public Library, Fr.F.v.XIV, fol. 101v.

The Tree of Jesse, in turn, was adapted to fit a genuine dream motif in the illustrations to the *Roman de la Rose*. The dreamer of the prologue of the *Roman* is lying in bed, while the rose tree grows like the tree of Jesse in the background (Fig. 6). Thanks to the convention of cyclical contiguity the reader knows that all the pictures following the dream scene represent the content of the dream. The dreamer of the *Roman de la Rose* is also related to the author portraits to be discussed further below (Figs. 22-27).[8]

Combinations of juxtaposition and cyclic contiguity proved particularly useful for illustrating difficult literary narratives. A thirteenth-century illuminator used these devices for the story of the monk and the Virgin in Gautier de Coincy's *Miracles de Nostre Dame* (Fig. 7). In the Leningrad manuscript the monk is first seen at nightly prayer to the sculpture of the Virgin. Then the Virgin visits him in a dream, showing him a splendidly decorated book with the text of Isaiah. She also allows the monk to kiss her cheek. The last scene shows the monk being chastised for his sleepiness on the following day. The two dream scenes stand out thanks to their elaborate background. The conventionally recumbent figure again serves to indicate that this is a dream scene, while the content of the dream is shown in the third square. The manuscript thus differentiates two phases of the dream that are fused into a single picture in another manuscript, the *Miracles* in the Bibliothèque Nationale (ms.fr. 25532, Fig. 8).

A few words should perhaps be said here about medieval dream theories. Scholasticism had adopted Macrobius's division of dreams into five main types. Judged according to this normative classification the nightly vision of Gautier's monk would have been of slight value.[9] On the whole finer points of theology did not apply to the popular tradition of miracles on which Gautier based his poem. But on one issue scholastic psychology and popular belief agreed: dreams, even if occasioned by the dreamer's daytime experiences, may still be genuine visions by which the Lord and the saints appear to ordinary mortals. Or, applied to our *exemplum,* the fact that the monk's dream derived from his intensive preoccupation with a sculpture did not deprive the dream of its divine origin: the Virgin had indeed condescended to appear to

---

[8] For the adaptation for the Roman de la Rose, see Alfred Kuhn, "Die Illustration des Rosenromans" (*Jahr. d. kunsthist. Samml. d. allerh. Kaiserhauses,* 31, 1913, pp. 1-66), p. 22. Also: John V. Fleming, *The Roman de la Rose, A Study in Allegory and Iconography,* Princeton 1969, p. 37.

[9] Macrobius, *Commentary on the Dream of Scipio,* tr. with an introd. a. notes by W. H. Stahl, New York 1952, Ch. III and Introd. pp. 41, 53. Honorius of Autun (J. P. Migne, *Patrologia latina,* 172, col. 1163) distinguished between dreams coming from God, from the Devil and from the dreamer's own thoughts and experiences.

Fig. 8. The monk's vision. Gautier de Coincy, Miracles de Nostre Dame,
Bibliothèque Nationale, Ms.fr. 25532, fol. 66r (Photo Bibl. Nat.).

her little servant. In fact there was no hard-and-fast distinction between different kinds of visions such as dreams, appearances of the Lord and the saints,
and the inner experiences achieved in contemplative mysticism.[10]

In addition to the simple form of juxtaposition discussed so far, we find a
variation of the method making it possible to depict what a person D is
supposing another person A to be. Here, again, pictorial narrative strived to
emulate verbal narrative where a writer could describe the situation by using
words such as 'supposing to be', 'mistaking for', 'recognizing as' and the like.
In the religious cycles it was, above all, Christ's appearences after Resurrection that taxed the ingenuity of the painters and sculptors.

Up to the thirteenth century the *Noli me tangere* had been depicted in a
simple, straightforward way with the resurrected Saviour standing in front of a
kneeling Mary Magdalen. But if read carefully the Gospel text contained a

[10] Sixten Ringbom, "Devotional Images and Imaginative Devotions" (*Gaz. des Beaux-Arts,*
VI:73, 1969, pp. 159-170).

Fig. 9. Noli me tangere. Detail from a French 14th-c. retable, Musée de Cluny, Cl.10838 (Photo Service Photographique).

challenge to the artist. Might it be possible to suggest the fact that Mary Magdalen first takes the suddenly appearing figure to be the gardener and only after a moment recognizes him as Christ? How does one, as it were, conceal Christ's identity from Mary Magdalen without concealing it from the beholder? This question was actually first posed in another medium, liturgical drama.

Some time during the late twelfth century the Easter plays incorporated the risen Christ. In its simplest form the appearing of Christ to Mary Magdalen was elaborated as an extension of the dramatic scene of the three Marys and the angel in the grave, the *Visitatio sepulchri*.[11] Here the priest, impersonating the Saviour, held a cross which he concealed from Mary Magdalen until the moment when he uttered the word "Maria!". As early as the thirteenth century stage instructions began to pay regard to the words of the Gospel: "existimans quia hortulanus esset" (John 20:15). A version of the *Visitatio sepulchri* thus contains the stage instruction "veniat quidam preparatus in similitudinem

[11] Karl Young, *The Drama of the Medieval Church*, vol. 1, Oxford 1951 (1933), p. 370.

Hortolani".[12] Yet more elaborate is the change of costume prescribed in a fifteenth-century text from Coutances: at first Christ enters "in habitu Ortolani", then leaves the stage to re-enter "as quickly as possible clad in a silk robe or pallium and holding a cross."[13] In a mime this is clearly an adequate method of suggesting Magdalen's mistake. But translated to pictorial terms such a change of costume would require two separate scenes of a cycle without really yielding a corresponding return in narrative thrust. This may have been one reason why the two phases of the episode were condensed into a single image, where Mary Magdalen's mistake is suggested by giving Christ the attributes of a gardener.

When and where this innovation was introduced into pictorial art is not quite clear; besides, it is possible that the figure of Christ as a gardener was adopted for the *Noli me tangere* by artists working independently of another. Émile Mâle pointed to a relief of 1351 in the choir of Notre Dame in Paris as the first instance of the motif where Christ holds a spade, while at the same time admitting that a version with Christ holding a hatchet was current in Sienese art already at the beginning of the fourteenth century.[14] A French Passion retable dated to the fourteenth century (Musée de Cluny, Cl. 10838) also features the motif of the spade (Fig. 9). Somewhat doubtful is the object held by Christ in the moralized Bible; it is not a cross, nor does it look like a gardener's tool, but it does not at least refer to Christ as directly as a cross would do (Fig. 10).

The idea of suggesting Mary Magdalen's mistake may also have been inspired by the older motif of Christ as a pilgrim, that is, the theatrical costume introduced in order to show what Christ's companions thought about the stranger during the journey to Emmaus and the supper in the inn. Pächt called attention to a North French Book of homilies in Cambrai as containing one of the earliest instances of the motif, which also recurs in the St. Albans Psalter (Fig. 11).[15] The famous Christ as a Pilgrim in San Domingo de Silos is more or

[12] Young, vol 1, p. 395. A twelfth-century play already refers to the figure of Christ as "Ortolanus", *ibid.* p. 681.

[13] Young, vol, 1, p. 409. – Curiously enough, Pseudo-Bonaventure does not exploit Mary Magdalen's mistake, see *Meditations on the Life of Christ,* transl. Isa Ragusa & Rosalie B. Green, Princeton 1961, ch. LXXXVIII.

[14] Emile Male, *L'art religieux de la fin du moyen âge en France,* 5. ed., Paris 1949, p. 77, fig. 39. G. Schiller, *Ikonographie...* Bd.3, 1971, pp. 97f. Mâle adduced fifteenth-century plays by Gréban and Jean-Michel, but, as pointed out above, Mary Magdalen's mistake is already elaborated by thirteenth-century plays.

[15] Pächt, p. 35.

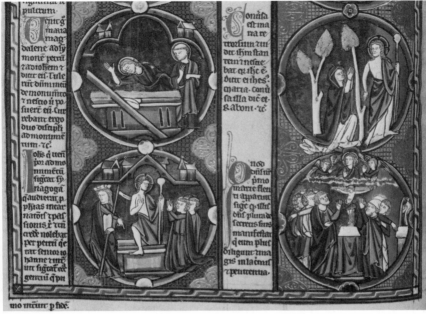

Fig. 10. Noli me tangere; The resurrection. Bible moralisée, The British Library, MS. Harley 1527, fol. 59v, *detail*. (Photo The British Library).

Fig. 11. The supper at Emmaus. St. Albans Psalter, Hildesheim, St. Gotthard, p. 70 (Photo The Warburg Institute Photographic Collection).

less contemporary with the Cambrai manuscript and may be an independent development also inspired by liturgical drama where, as a matter of course, Christ is referred to as *peregrinus*.[16] Nor is it absolutely necessary to assume inspiration from drama since in the Vulgate text Christ is actually addressed: Tu solus peregrinus es in Jerusalem (Luke 24:18). Both Christ as a pilgrim and Christ as a gardener remained popular motifs down to the end of the Middle Ages.

Now, the subjective experiences of a protagonist may also be conveyed to the beholder even without resorting to theatrical attire or attributes. A modification of the scale or size of a figure may just as well suggest how a protagonist interprets what she or he sees. A case in point is the so-called *Pietà corpusculum:* among the various types of the *Pietà* motif there is one group of sculptures in which the dead Christ in the Virgin's lap is the size of a small child (Fig. 12).[17] The meaning of this image would be clear enough even without the textual evidence that we happen to possess. It shows us the Virgin dreamily recalling a time long ago when Jesus was an infant dressed in swaddling-clothes instead of the shroud or the loin-cloth of the dead Saviour. Christ has been reduced to child-size as a visualization of the Virgin's thoughts; the beholder is invited to share, as it were, her melancholy recollections of the days back in Bethlehem.

The method which we have called juxtaposition does not distinguish between levels of reality; dreamer and dream are depicted in the same pictorial space. Similarly Christ's spade, hatchet or pilgrim's dress are as tangible as any other object in the picture: there seems to be no practicable method of suggesting that Christ merely *appears* to be carrying a spade without *actually* doing so.

But for certain subjects the medieval artist knew how to suggest different orders of reality. This brings us to the fifth method in our list: *differentiation.* The differentiation of levels is a time-honoured convention for defining the regions of heaven and earth: the heavenly region is separated from the earthly region by means of a cloud frill, a strip of more or less stylized cloud patterns. Since true visions were of heavenly origin it appeared natural to represent them as extensions of the higher regions. Hence the cloud patterns which could be used together or alternatively with other visionary motifs: light halos,

---

[16] Young, vol. 1, pp. 459, 463 ("se fingens Peregrinum"), 471.

[17] For this motif, see Male, p. 128, and Wolfgang Krönig, "Rheinische Vesperbilder aus Leder und ihr Umkreis" (*Wallraf-Richartz-Jahrbuch*, XXIV, 1962, pp. 96-192), pp. 104, 163f.

Fig. 12. Pietà from Lappi Church, ca. 1450. Museum, Rauma (Photo P.O. Welin, The Finnish Museum Authority).

Fig. 13. Ezechiel's Vision
(Ezech, 8:2) with moralization.
Bible moralisée, Bibliothèque
Nationale, Ms. lat. 11560, fol. 197v,
detail (Photo Bibl. Nat.).

rays of light and mandorlas. Both light and cloud patterns agreed with numerous scriptural passages describing visions.

The moralized Bible again illustrates the ingenuity with which the thirteenth-century illuminator used this pictorial vocabulary. Throughout the manuscript the cloud-frill has the traditional function of marking the borderline between heaven and earth across which the Lord makes himself known to man. When God appears in a vision proper, the cloud border may even be stretched to a vesicular shape, a form representing, as it were, a temporary extension of heaven to the earthly level. The cloud pattern becomes a halo or a mandorla surrounding the figure of God when he appears in a vision (Fig. 13).

In the course of time the original, more strict meaning of the cloud frill as well as the other types of halos became diluted. The moralized Bible already offers instances of a loose usage of halos and cloud frills. In the illustration to Exodus Ch. 26 (Fig. 14) the border becomes a pictorial quotation mark, a

Fig. 14. The Lord speaking to Moses (Exod. ch. 26) with moralization: Christ teaching his followers. Bible moralisée, Oxford, Bodleian Library MS 270b, fol. 53v, *detail* (Photo Bodleian Library).

visual equivalent for the *dixit* of the caption ("Dixit dominus ad Moysen: Inspice et fac omnia secundum exemplar quod tibi ostensum est in monte"). The talk balloon function is equally marked in the moralization contained in the following medallion where Christ is teaching and referring to the examples set by the holy fathers.

Now, even false visions such as the phantasms of pagans were represented by means of halos and cloud frills. The earliest instance of this usage that I have found comes from a French *Cité de Dieu* of 1376 (Fig. 15). The religion of the pagans is depicted with the same formal accessories as Christian religion, but instead of Christ and the saints we have conventionally shaped idols and devilish demons appearing in the sky. The two types of pagan gods apparently reflect the illuminator's wish to visualize St. Augustine's account of pagan dualism which takes up the text portion; some of the ancient gods were considered good, others bad.

A special type of halo is connected with the Virgin on the crescent or the

Fig. 15. Pagans adoring their gods. St. Augustine, Cité de Dieu, Bibliothèque Nationale, Ms.fr.
22912, fol. 384r (Photo Bibl.Nat.)

Maria in Sole, as she was sometimes called in the fifteenth century. Originally
derived from the iconography of the book of Revelation, the *mulier amicta sole*
was made to serve in other iconographic contexts, too. The immaculists of the
fifteenth century, for instance, adopted the motif for their propaganda in the
image of the Immaculate Virgin. The Virgin on the Crescent was also found
convenient for representing the vision shown to Emperor Augustus by the
Tiburtine Sibyl, since according to the Golden Legend the Virgin appeared to
the Emperor in the middle of a golden halo surrounding the sun.[18]

It would seem that the significance of the Maria in Sole became less and less
distinct; worn down, as it were, in frequent use for widely different contexts.
This is why lesser potentates than emperor Augustus could also be portrayed
contemplating a vision of the Virgin in the Sun. The Book of Hours of the
Maréchal de Boucicaut shows the owner of the book and his wife praying to

[18] Jacobus de Voragine, *Die Legenda aurea,* übers. von Richard Benz, Heidelberg, n.d., p. 52.

Fig. 16. Le Maréchal de Boucicaut and his wife. Heures du Marechal de Boucicaut, Paris, Mus. Jacquemart-André, fol. 26v (Photo Bulloz).

the Virgin appearing in the midst of saints (Fig. 16). In the prayerbook of James IV of Scotland Queen Margaret is seen directing her devotion to the Virgin on the Crescent (Fig. 18). Neither miniature depicts a vision in the sense of an apparition. Instead the arrangement is intended to convey the impression of a mental image of the kind that played such an important role in late medieval mysticism and especially in lay piety. In medieval psychology such mental images were characteristic of inner sight, sometimes referred to as *visio spiritualis,* sometimes as *visio imaginaria.* The spiritual vision was superior to ordi-

Figs. 17-18. King James and Queen Margaret at prayer. Prayer-Book of James IV,
Österreichische Nationalbibliothek, Cod. 1897, fol. 24v and 243r (Photo Bildarchiv
d. Öst. Nationalbibl.).

Fig. 19 Georg Pencz,
Joseph telling about his
dreams. Woodcut 1544.
(Photo Konsthist. Inst.,
Åbo Akademi).

nary sight *(visio corporalis)* but inferior to the intellectual vision *(visio intellectualis)* of the mystics, which did not make use of images.[19]

Ordinary or corporeal sight is depicted in the companion portrait of King James's prayerbook which shows the king himself in devotion before a painted image of Christ (Fig. 17). But in both cases the image, whether corporeal or spiritual, has a double reference. On the one hand the image forms an extension of the eternal into the temporal world, and on the other hand it suggests

[19] See note 10 above, and Ringbom, "Maria in sole and the Virgin of the Rosary" (*Journal of the Warburg & Courtauld Institutes,* vol. 25, 1962, nos. 3-4, pp. 326-330).

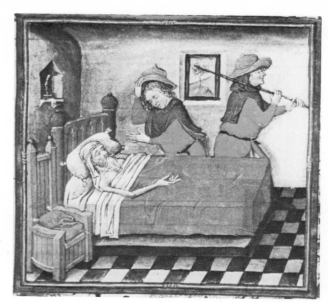

Fig. 20. The dying Adam dispatching Seth to Paradise. The Hours of Catherine of Cleves, New York, The Pierpont Morgan Library, M.917, p.75 (After J. Plummer, *The Hours of C.o.C.*, 1966, pl.79).

to the beholder what is going on in the minds of the king and the queen; or rather, perhaps, an exhortation to the owners to think devoutly on the Saviour and the Virgin.

With the miniature of James IV we have also reached the last of the pictorial devices listed in our table. According to the present interpretation the panel serves to show what the king is contemplating on. We shall name this method *appendage* of a subordinate motif. The subordinate motif may be appended in different ways; as an 'image in the image', or enclosed in a window aperture as in Georg Pencz's woodcut *Joseph telling his dreams,* where the sheaves, the sun, moon and stars are convincingly integrated into the background land-scape (Fig. 19). In either case some kind of framework separates the motif from the main representation. Pencz's woodcut is dated as late as 1544, but the device was known much earlier. In the Hours of Catherine of Cleves the win-dow view indicates what the dying Adam is telling Seth to do: that is, to go and fetch a branch of the tree of grace in Paradise.[20] In this continuous narrative Seth is already striding to the door in order to carry out his father's wish (Fig. 20).

[20] *The Hours of Catherine of Cleves,* Introd. and comm. by John Plummer, London 1966, p. 79.

Fig. 21. Pharaoh's dream. Lubeck Bible of 1494 (After Schramm, XI:967).

Normally the subordinate motif was given some ostensible motivation or pretext. The earliest instance of an appended image lacking every such pretext that I have been able to find comes from the Lübeck Bible of 1494 where Pharaoh's dreams are contained in four plainly outlined circles (Fig. 21). Although there are no frames or frills in the woodcut, its stage setting is not left entirely unaffected by the introduction of the circles: each roundel is set against its own, distinctly marked portion of the background walls. We sense that the draughtsman has hesitated to place the circles in the arbitrary or haphazard manner of the modern strip cartoonist.

The four pictorial conventions for the recounting of thoughts and experiences, which I have dealt with here, were often used two or more at a time. Sometimes indeed the narrative structure became so complex and ingenious that the image would remain completely unintelligible but for the accompanying text.

Generations of artists from the fourteenth century to the present day have regarded Dante's *Divine Comedy* as the touchstone of the illustrator's skill. The *Paradiso,* in particular, has been regarded as more or less defying illustration. It is characteristic that only from the fifteenth century onwards illustrators succeeded in suggesting the different narrative levels of Dante's text – indeed it may be asked whether this feat has been accomplished ever since. One of the

Fig. 22. Dante, Beatrice and Folco of Marseilles. Divina Commedia, The British Library, MS. Yates Thompson 36, fol. 145r (Photo The British Library).

most successful illustrators, Giovanni di Paolo, working in Florence around 1450, used both juxtaposition and differentiation when he visualized the colourful but abstruse diction of the *Paradiso*. The illustration to Canto IX (Fig. 22) shows Dante and Beatrice hovering in space in front of two blessed souls that are floating about as lights. The woman in the halo is Cunizza, who in the previous miniature had been depicted as delivering her speech on the perils of the wars between the city states. The man in a Cistercian robe and bishop's mitre is Folco or Foulques of Marseilles, sometime troubadour and later to become bishop of Toulouse. Folco reflects on his earthly and spiritual love and ends with an accusation of Florence, where the Devil is seen handing out bribes to popes and cardinals. Florence is easily recognized thanks to the fleur-de-lys and its famous buildings.[21]

The main scenery, that is the city set against a background of Tuscan hills, is the subject matter of the speech delivered by Folco who is set apart from this content by his radiant, golden halo. If compared with the examples discussed so far, content and speaker have here changed places, whereas Folco's audience, Beatrice and Dante, move in the picture space of Folco's story; the

---

[21] Peter Brieger, Millard Meiss, Charles S. Singleton, *Illuminated Manuscripts of the Divine Comedy*, Vol. I-II, Princeton 1969, vol. I, pp. 188-189.

Fig. 23. Flemish, ca 1470, Valerius Maximus. Bratislava, City Library (After F. Winkler, *Die flämische Buchmalerei*, 1925, pl.45).

listeners are thus juxtaposed with the content of the speech. The reason for this arrangement is, of course, the fact that the text requires Folco to be sur-rounded by radiant light. Now, Giovanni di Paolo was also capable of adapting the structure to the varying requirements of the text, as shown, for instance, by the miniatures illustrating Cantos VI-VII. In the first scene Beatrice and Dante had conversed with emperor Justinian, and in the next scene the emperor is still seen hovering in the air because Dante is reflecting on one of the remarks that Justinian had made. Three scenes depicting the Fall of Man, Annunciation and Crucifixion are here intended to epitomize the long theological discourse on salvation delivered by Beatrice.[22]

Giovanni di Paolo's illustrations are formally related to an iconographical speciality sometimes referred to with the German term *Assistenzporträt,* that is, at picture featuring the artist or author, as the case may be, integrated with the action. Since the author *Assistenzporträt* makes use of the pictorial devices dealt with above it deserves attention in our context. Thus juxtaposition is used in a Flemish Valerius Maximus manuscript illuminated ca. 1470 (Fig. 23). The author and his patron, the emperor Tiberius, witness the scenes described, discreetly looking through a window or standing in a doorway. Juxtaposition is appropriate enough for illustrating a factual text or a collection of anecdotes such as Valerius Maximus, whereas a text originating in a vision or revelation is more adequately epitomized by the method we have called differentiation. Hence the lavish use of cloud frills in apocalyptic imagery. The traditional rendering of St. John on the island of Pathmos receiving his revelation became a norm and a model for the iconography of lesser visionaries, too. Revelations as different as the rather private visions of St. Hildegard of Bingen and the celestial hierarchy purported to have been revealed to St. Dionysius fitted into the same formula (Figs. 24-25).

The appendage of subordinate motifs, again, seems to have been suitable for works without claims to divine inspiration. In a Flemish Boëtius manuscript of 1476 the consolation of philosophy is depicted on a painting hanging on the wall of the armarium, where the author is sitting with his book (Fig. 26). The framed picture, which is of a very unusual size for the late fifteenth century, shows Dame Philosophy consoling a sick man lying in his bed. – And what shall we say about the inhabited scroll growing out from the book in the frontispiece of Johann Froben's editions of the *Decretales* of Gregory IX and the *Liber sextus decretalium* of Boniface VIII? It is no doubt an ingenious, but perhaps a little far-fetched solution to the task of visualizing the decrees that the pope is issuing to the judiciary. Two medallions contain court scenes, one murder, theft and adultery, one the celebration of Mass and one the rites of marriage (Fig. 27).

---

[22] *Ibid.* pls. 444a and 445c.

Fig. 24. The Seventh Vision of Hildegard von Bingen. Liber divinorum operum, Lucca, Biblioteca governativa, Cod. 1942 (After H.v.B., *Welt und Mensch,* ed. H. Schipperges, 1965, pl. 10).

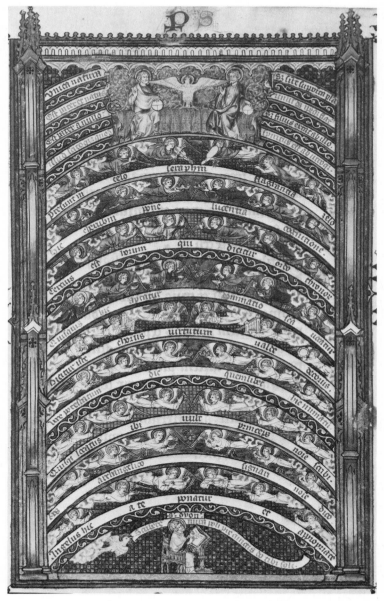

Fig. 25. The celestial hierarchy. Légende de St. Dénis, Bibliothèque Nationale, Ms.fr. 2090, fol. 107v (Photo Bibl.Nat.).

Fig. 26. Boetius, De consolatione philosophiae. The British Library, MS. Harley 4335, fol. 1r (Photo The British Library).

Fig. 27. Frontispiece to Decretales of Gregory IX, Basel, Joh. Froben 1494 (After Schramm, XXII: 1107).

Most of the instances discussed above have a complex pictorial structure, and many would be difficult or impossible to understand without the help of a caption or an accompanying text. Sometimes they appear so contrived that the formal means seem to belie the original end of telling a story. We know why it came to be like this, and we have come here to Odense to discuss the matter: this was one of the effects that the medieval narrative tradition had upon medieval iconography. But despite the ingenuity and the efforts lavished on them, many of the representations still fail to convey more than a sample of the literary material that they illustrate, a mere outline tracing of the narrative plot. Nor could more be done: painting is a kind of mime or dumb show, whereas the span of the literary narrative can be enormously wide. This, it may be added, is one of the reasons why European art gradually freed itself from the literary model.

The effect of the narrative tradition, then, was not always an entirely beneficial one; the art of illustration practised by, say, Giovanni di Paolo clearly represented a dead end in the historical evolution. What really mattered was that the challenge from the literary media resulted in experiments with pictorial devices. Indeed, much fifteenth-century art deserves the description 'experimental' infinitely better than much of the dogmatic activities that have later been marketed with this label. Many of the experiments did not invite repetition, but others were thoroughly successful and became part of the pictorial idiom from the Renaissance down to our own day. Also, some of our contemporary picture media such as the motion picture still seem to labour under the same tyranny of literature that once ruled over medieval art. Since the invention of the sound-track film is no longer, as painting always was, a dumb show – but this makes no fundamental difference since in the movie the spoken word rather equals the text scrolls and legends of medieval art. To the contemporary film maker the problem which we have discussed here is still a very real one. For how does one *visualize* a person's dreams, recollections, fantasies, thoughts, not to mention lies, in a film? How would Buñuel stage the *Noli me tangere?* Or Ingmar Bergman the lies that Putiphar's wife told about the young Joseph? As we know, even a modestly plausible rendering of such things even today ensures praise and fame to the film director. If studied closely enough many of these devices prove to be quite similar to the ones we have met in medieval illustration.

Åbo Academy

"Triumph" as a motif in the poems of Petrarch and in contemporary and later art

by Esther Nyholm

Petrarch's *Triumphs* is not only that work of his which has been most illustrated, but also that which, through an analytical study of its imagery confronted with its motifs, provides the best opportunity of seeing Petrarch's relationship to the Middle Ages and the Renaissance. The application to literature of principles taken from art history will be useful here.

Petrarch was very interested in the art of his time. During his years in Avignon, he was a close friend of Simone Martini. It is said that Simone Martini painted a portrait of Laura. (If only it could be found, the literary historians would stop wondering about whether she did exist!) He also drew a cover illustration for Petrarch's Virgil manuscript and this has been preserved, though in a somewhat faded condition (Fig. 1). This picture shows no knowledge at all of the classical tradition. Virgil is depicted as a dreamy French poet of the Middle Ages, and the few attempts to give the picture a classical look are hardly successful. There is, for example, very little of the hero about Aeneas. Nonetheless, Petrarch looked after this illustration carefully. It was the work of one of the greatest artist of his time, and this was more important to him than the fact that it did not really suit the subject matter.

Petrarch also had a great regard for Giotto, another contemporary artist, although he could hardly have known him personally. Giotto died in 1337 and though Petrarch was born in 1304, sufficient is known about his movements up until the year of Giotto's death almost certainly to rule out a meeting between them. But Petrarch owned one of Giotto's paintings, a painting he made special mention of in his will, leaving it to someone who would value and enjoy it. Petrarch died in 1374. If one did not know that the popularity as an artist Giotto had enjoyed during his lifetime had already begun to wane, it would be possible to gather this from Petrarch's will. We do not know which painting Petrarch owned or whether it was a genuine Giotto, but that is of minor importance. It is Petrarch's admiration for the artist that is of significance. It was more than a passive admiration, as the *Triumphs* illustrate. In "Triumphus

Fig. 1. Simone Martini, Frontispiece for Virgil Manuscript, Milano, Biblioteca Ambrosiana.

Fig. 2. Giotto, The Vision of St Francis. Assisi, the Church of St Francis.

Cupidinis", Petrarch has Cupid drive a chariot of fire, obviously inspired either by the chariot of fire Giotto painted Elijah in, in the chapel of Scrovegni in Padua, or by the one St Francis appears in before his praying disciples, painted in the church of St Francis in Assisi (Fig. 2). Petrarch had apparently seen these paintings, although the only important works of Giotto which he mentions are the frescoes in Naples.

When writers make a great deal of use of pictures in their writing, there is a tendency to imagine that they are also painters. There is, for example, a story about Dante. Sitting thinking about Betarice on the anniversary of her death, with a pencil in his hand, he suddenly began to draw an angel. There is no corresponding account of a Laura-angel drawn by Petrarch, but there are some hasty landscape sketches in the margin of some of his manuscripts which could be his own. They are good without being exceptional.

Petrarch wrote his *Triumphs* over many years. Agreement cannot be reached on exactly how long it took him, but they are amongst his last works. They are remarkable in that they all have Latin titles but are written in Italian. Only about one twentieth of the large amount of written material which Petrarch left was written in Italian, with *Il Canzoniere* by far the best. *I Trionfi,* written in "terza rima" like the *Divine Comedy,* is not of the same standard

Fig. 3. Triumph, the Arch of Titus, Rome.

poetically, but it has a dramatic theme related in a dramatic way. It has therefore been a source of inspiration to many artists.

Altogether there are six Triumphs. They are sections of a whole, one Triumph replacing another. The victor of one Triumph is defeated in the next, while the final Triumph cancels all those preceding. It is important to remember that this continuity exists, because when one studies the paintings which the Triumphs inspired, it is often difficult to see this continuity.

The first Triumph is called "Triumphus Cupidinis", the triumph of Cupid. It starts with the poet reclining beneath a tree in a forest – Simone Martini's depiction of the poet Virgil comes to mind – and while his thoughts are occupied with his first meeting with Laura, he falls asleep. He dreams that he sees Cupid driving his fiery chariot drawn by four horses "whiter than snow". He has a bow in his hand, arrows by his side but neither armour nor shield – Petrarch mentions this explicitly. All he has is "wings of a thousand colours". Around his chariot there are a crowd of people, either wounded, dead or taken captive. Petrarch looks in vain for a face he knows, but sufferings have distorted every one. He is addressed by someone he does not recognize, who proves to be one of his closest friends. The identity of this friend has been the source of a great deal of discussion and disagreement, but his purpose here is the same as Virgil's in the *Divine Comedy:* he is to point out the various people in the throng to Petrarch. The friend says that he has been expecting him, Petrarch explains the state of his feelings, and the friend remarks "O figliuol mio, qual per te fiamma è accesa" (what a flame ignited for you). The friend describes Cupid as a frightful master, a vice, "Ei nacque d'ozio e di lascivia umana, nudrito di pensier dolci soavi, fatto signor e dio di gente vana" (made master and god by thoughtless people). At the head of the throng is Caesar, hopelessly blinded by Cleopatra. After him other Roman emperors follow, including Augustus and Nero. They in turn are followed by mythological figures in couples – Jason and Medea, Mars and Venus. Masinissa and Sophnisba are described in detail, and Petrarch addresses himself to them. Then Odysseus is seen, followed by Old Testament characters and some from recent times, including Paolo and Francesca. Laura appears standing all alone, like a picture in a dream within his own dream. He notices that Cupid fears her.

The procession continues. He now sees the classical poets, Dante and Beatrice, Socrates and many others. The procession moves forward through the world "with people from Thule and India", and finally reaches Cyprus, the home of Venus, Cupid's mother. It passes through a triumphal arch decorated with dreams, vague impressions and distorted opinions. At the end of this poem the procession is depicted as "an enormous painting seen in a brief moment" (quasi lunga pittura in tempo breve).

Looking more closely at the imagery used in this Triumph, one can see that parts have been taken from literature and art, from antiquity and contemporary sources. A Roman Triumphal March is without doubt its main inspiration. Petrarch says himself of Caesar "or di lui si trionfa" (now he is the victim in the triumphal march). Petrarch derives his description of the Triumphal March from classical writers, like Pliny. He calls it "questa danza" (this dance), an expression which brings to mind troubadour songs, which he knew so well from France. The procession through the Triumphal Arch on Cyprus is part of the classical aspect of this procession. A triumphal arch did exist as a permanent building in Rome: it probably was to be found on Campus Martius. All processions of triumph passed through it. Petrarch had seen triumphal arches still in existence during his visit to Rome: he has given descriptions of them and of other classical monuments. He had seen reliefs of the triumphal marches of Marcus Aurelius and Titus, with the chariot drawn by four horses (Fig. 3). The reason for this becoming a chariot of fire in Petrarch's version may be found in the influence of Giotto's paintings, as already mentioned. He

Fig. 4. Vices, Miniature from Hortus & Deliciarum, ca. 1170 (from van Marle, *Iconographie de l'art profane ou Moyen Age et à la Renaissance*, La Haye, 1932, p. 76).

has an additional reason for the change, for he mentions the flames by which Cupid causes his victims to be consumed. It is important to note that Petrarch does not allow his work to be dominated by the classical ideal but reshapes it to suit his own purposes, inspired by contemporary art.

Pictorial representations of Cupid being drawn in a chariot were not unknown in antiquity, as evidenced by a medal with his motif, in the Palazzo Medici Riccardi in Florence, copied by Donatello in the fifteenth century. But apart from this, Petrarch could have found inspiration somewhere else, especially as regards his interpretation of Cupid as having a cruel nature.

Here, though, it is necessary to break in with a few remarks about Cupid. Originally he was a peaceful, winged creature accompanying his mother, Venus. This is the way he was portrayed until the fourth century B.C. But suddenly Cupid began to appear with a bow, Euripides apparently being the first to describe him thus. From this point Cupid began to develop his own personality. Generally, and especially during the Middle Ages, he was not considered to use his talents in the cause of good.[1] A manuscript from the twelfth century, for example, shows an illustration of Cupid in a large chariot together with other Vices (Fig. 4).[2] A point of particular interest about this illustration is that here Cupid has both armour and shield. Petrarch, by remarking that his Cupid was not furnished with these, made it clear that he knew that this was out of pattern. On the other hand, Petrarch's Cupid was decorated with wings of a thousand colours. Here our thoughts are immediately led to the Byzantine paintings where the angels have similar wings. No doubt Petrarch had seen a variation on this theme in Rome, as about 1300 Pietro Cavallini decorated the Church of St Cecilia in Rome with mosaics and frescoes and here we find flocks of angels with multicoloured wings (Fig. 5). Consequently, in his description of Cupid, Petrarch has mixed elements from classical art and from the art of his own time. He knows that he is changing a well-known tradition when he depicts Cupid naked, but here the classical model is predomination, while on the other hand, he chooses a medieval model for the wings of Cupid.

The first of the Triumphs described a real Triumphal March, but this is not

---

[1] For the description of Cupid in the Roman period, the Middle Ages and the Renaissance see E. Panofsky, Blind Cupid, in *Studies in Iconology*, London 1972, pp. 95-128. A connection between Petrarch and Francesco Barberino as proposed by Panofsky is rather questionable. One might find a parallel between the zeal of both authors to explain their description of Cupid as differing from the traditional one.

[2] See R. van Marle, *Iconogaphie de l'art profane au Moyen Age et à la Renaissance*. La Haye, 1932. II. p. 76.

Fig. 5. Pietro Cavallini, Angels. Santa Maria di Trastevere, Rome.

the case with the second, *Triumphus Pudicitie,* The Triumph of virtue. Here
there is no form of triumphal chariot but on the other hand other characteristics associated with a Roman Triumphal March are used. The poem begins
with Petrarch's philosophical thoughts concerning the comfort he gains from
seeing divine persons suffer the agonies of love. If *they* have to give in to
Cupid, he can hardly hope to escape. But Cupid is unable to crush Laura. This
was apparent in the First Triumph but the actual battle between Cupid and
Laura is described in the second Triumph. They fight as fiercely as lions. The
noise is so deafening that it would drown even the sound of Etna in eruption.
Petrarch is certain that Cupid will win: this is what experience leads us to
expect, but "Virtue which does not desert the good" places herself between
Cupid and Laura and diverts his arrows. Petrarch still hopes that Cupid will
win: then he will be able to be united with Laura. But an army of Virtues join
in the battle and, one by one, they take away the victims surrounding Cupid.
His power is taken from him: he is bound: and his fall is compared with Hanni-
bal's or Goliath's. His sheath and arrows are destroyed, the feathers pulled out
of his wings. Now virtuous women join the Virtues, women who, in mythology,
the Bible or in history have been remembered for their virtue. This throng of
people (Petrarch calls it here "il trionfo"), proceeds from Cyprus, where
Cupid's triumphal march ends, to distant parts. Their goal is Rome and the
temple of Venus Pudicitia. Laura, the beautiful victrix, lays a crown of laurels
on Venus' statue in the same way that the Roman *triumphator* laid his on Jupiter's statue on the Capitol. Cupid is guarded by several young men who have
also shown a virtuous nature. Petrarch is told who they are by his guide, still
accompanying him.

   This summary makes it clear that in this section of the poem, the relation to
the classical triumphal march is much more complicated than it was in the
first. A battle is followed by a procession, with the defeated enemy in captivity.
This procession Petrarch calls "il trionfo". When the procession reaches its
end a crown of victory is placed on the statue of the goddess whose name is
also in the title of the poem. In the battle Laura is her representative or her
incarnation. Laura has triumphed, a triumph described in a drama in three
acts: the fight, the procession, the wreath-laying. It would be difficult to
include a triumphal chariot in this composition.

   One may regard this section as an interesting commentary on the classical
triumphal march. Some have regarded the triumphant Roman emperor as the
incarnation of Jupiter at the foot of whose statue he lays his wreath. The

emperor is seen to represent Jupiter, in the same way as Laura here represents Venus Pudicitia.

The next section, "Triumphus Mortis", the triumph of death, shows close connections both with antiquity and the Middle Ages. It is a known fact that a slave sat behind the caesar on the triumphal chariot continuously whispering in his ear "hominem te esse memento", remember you are only human. Immediately after Laura has been portrayed as "la bella vincitrice" (the beautiful victrix), we are told that she is made only "of spirit and a little dust" (ignudo spirito e poca terra).

Petrarch describes how Laura and her following of young maidens on their way back from Rome – one is reminded of Saint Ursula and her 11,000 virgins returning from their pilgrimage to the Pope – meet a woman dressed in black, who rushes towards them like a fury. She introduces herself and tells of her strength – she has defeated the Greeks, the Trojans and finally the Romans. And now she will attack this throng of people, right at the moment when life seems happiest. Laura replies that Death can only take her body, thus implying that its triumph cannot be complete. What is more, others, especially Petrarch, will mourn her death more than she will be able to herself. In other words, Death cannot triumph over Laura. Death makes Laura look out over the countryside. Wherever she looks, dead popes, kings and dukes are to be seen, their wealth and happiness taken from them. Petrarch leaves his philosophical thoughts on death to regard Laura's death as it actually occurred. The event is particularized: the date of her death, 6th April, given. After several days of raging fever she passes away, surrounded by the young maidens who are her friends. Laura expires like a flame that dies out of its own accord, not like a flame extinguished by force. The description of the dead Laura is extremely poetic and in contrast to the dramatic tone of the battle with Cupid. The night after Laura dies, she appears in a dream to Petrarch. Sitting under a bay tree and a beech tree they converse. She says that it is she who is alive, he who is dead. At daybreak they have to part. Aurora brings daylight back to the mortal. Laura gives Petrarch the sad news that he will live for many years without her, "Al creder mio, tu starai in terra senza me gran tempo".

If one compares this triumph with the classical one, it becomes apparent that there are even fewer points of similarity here than in the preceding one. Nor does Petrarch refer to this part of the poem as "un trionfo". In this section, it is rather a question of an apparent triumph. Death marks the division between the living and the dead. In the first two sections of the poem ideas concerned with life have been depicted, while the last three sections are concerned with death and its aftermath. In itself, death cannot be said to represent a triumph over life. As Laura says herself, only her body disappears. In other words, virtue, a spiritual state, has not been vanquished by death.

It is difficult to establish where Petrarch derived the ideas he uses in describing death. Not from the art of antiquity, because Death was not worshipped, so Petrarch's idea of Death as a person would not have come from this source.[3] In Roman reliefs we find Death symbolized as putti, carrying torches pointing downwards. This symbolism is found again in medieval times, for example in a fresco in Campo Santo in Pisa, painted by an unknown artist called "il maestro del trionfo della morte", in the late fourteenth century, i. e. at about the same time as Petrarch wrote his Triumphs (Fig. 6). This fresco incidentally shows great similarity with the ideas Petrarch expressed, without necessarily implying that one directly influenced the other. There is the same representation of Death as a merciless force, striking down the happy and the wealthy. In this part of the fresco we can see Death ready to strike a group of young, carefree girls, similar to Petrarch's "bella schiera – beautiful throng". The title of this painting, "the triumph of death", is of a later date, so one cannot take this into consideration when making comparisons. One also has to be careful about interpreting, as some critics, expecially Millard Meiss, do, the paintings of Death's fierce destructiveness in this period as the result of the outbreak of the Plague in 1348, with its consequent frenzy of religious fear and repentance. This is said to have produced paintings intended to strike fear into the hearts of people looking at them, and painted in an old style as if it was feared that the modern style would not be sufficiently clear, or would appear too daring.[4] In his poem on the triumph of Death, Petrarch presents a different view, showing that death is not a punishment. His choice of subject matter is entirely a matter of philosophical considerations. Laura's death, also caused by the Plague, is only one aspect of the subject. In Pisa Death is portrayed as a skeleton, the form most common in medieval, renaissance and later times. Petrarch cannot, as far as we know, have been inspired to describe Death as a woman dressed in black from any contemporary sources. If anything, it reminds one of the goddesses of fate found in classical literature. In the triumph of Death there is no mention of a triumph. Petrarch uses the word in the title but in the poem itself there is no triumphal procession, or the laying of

---

[3] According to Pausanias, Polygnot is said to have represented Night, Sleep and Death on a relief. See J. Seznec, *The Survival of the Pagan Gods*. Princeton, 1972.

[4] See Millard Meiss, *Painting in Florence and Siena after the Black Death,* New York, 1964 (1951).

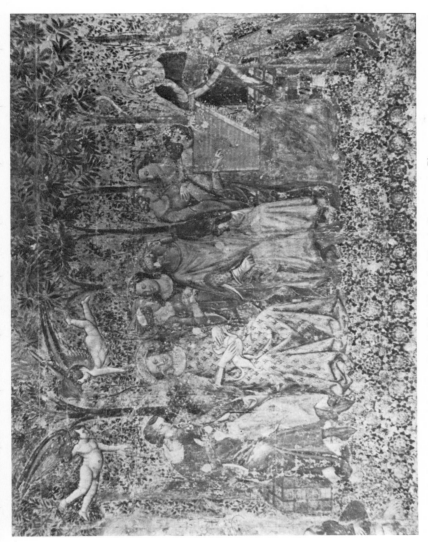

Fig. 6. Maestro del trionfo della morte, Detail of the Triumph of Death, Camposanto, Pisa.

a triumphal wreath. Once Death has triumphed over the human body, it disappears from the picture, and the rest of this section of the poem is wholly concerned with the discussion between Petrarch and Laura, which in itself signifies that Death is not a final point.

After the Triumph of Death follows *Triumphus Fame,* the Triumph of Fame. At this point the impression of watching a play in a theatre, or even of standing at the roadside watching a triumphal procession passing by, is strengthened. Death, which triumphed over Laura, who had triumphed over Petrarch, disappears to one side. Petrarch here uses the word "trionfare" meaning "to be stronger than, to conquer", to describe Death's and Laura's triumphs. As if coming in from the other side of a stage Fama enters, she who rescues mankind from the grave and gives him life, "quella che trae l'uom del sepolcro e'n vita il serba". She comes as a star, showing itself at dawn before the sun. Surprisingly enough, Petrarch gives up his attempt to describe her appearance, perhaps because so many descriptions are to be found in classical literature.[5] He even refers to the *rhetorical* portrayals of Fama in his phrase "di quali scole verrà 'l maestro che descriva a pieno quel ch'io vo' dir in semplici parole?", but he does not feel obliged to use any of them; his eyes are blinded by the morning light and it is impossible for him to distinguish her exact forms.

In this section of the poem Petrarch is surrounded by famous people who have the reason for their fame marked on their foreheads. He recognizes many who were victims of Cupid. Others are pointed out to Petrarch one by one – his guide is still present. They come forward in the same order as they once did on Via Sacra, Via Lata, on the Capitol, that is on the way which the Triumphal Procession followed in Rome. Here the characters are clearly arranged according to their rank or according to the rank Petrarch gives them. First of all, Petrarch's beloved Romans are seen, – their brows are marked with the word "Rome": they are followed by Greek conquerors of far–off tribes. Masinissa appears again, Abraham and David also file past. Petrarch becomes quite exhausted from seeing all these people but is refreshed at the sight of a group of beautiful women, including Cleopatra and Judith. Conquerors from times closer to his own appear – Charlemagne and Robert of Anjou. He is so absorbed in watching them that his guide has to prompt him to look to the other side. Here the philosophers, with Plato at their head, appear, followed by authors of antiquity, all identified by name. The poem breaks off suddenly. We are given no indication of where the procession is going. So one

---

[5] Virgil's description of Fame in book four of the Aeneid is the most famous in Roman literature.

cannot really relate this section to the classical triumphal procession. Fama is not depicted as the leader of the throng, and there is no sign of a triumphal chariot. In portraying Fame, Petrarch could have sought inspiration not only in literature, but also in classical or medieval art. Normally the figure is depicted as someone blowing a horn, but Petrarch prefers to let his characters reveal the reasons for their fame in person by letters on their foreheads, making the horn of Fama superfluous. If one compares this triumph with the first, Cupid's triumph, one can see, as an Italian critic has noted, that the first is a description of the triumph of the vanquished, "un trionfo dei trionfati", and the second a description of the triumph of the victors, "un trionfo dei trion-fanti".[6]

But that this is not the final disposition becomes clear in the next section, *Triumphus Temporis*. Here we meet Time who obliterates what Death could not obliterate, and Time is more powerful than Fame. This is the shortest of the poems, but it has a greater intensity than the others, suggesting the speed and strength of the passing of Time. The illusion that all the events described are part of Petrarch's dream is strengthened here. We have reached the moment of dawn, the moment of awakening, the moment when Time again becomes relevant. Fame was described as the Morning Star, appearing on the horizon just before the sun. But now the sun itself appears, for Time is described as the Sun, rising up and regarding Earth. He is angry that Fame has kept alive those people whom Death could not eradicate and that he himself has to bow down to Fame, even though he is powerful enough to drive the sun chariot with four horses over the ocean.

Having expressed his anger, Time flies off like a falcon looking for its prey, moving so fast that summer and winter, rosebuds and snowflakes follow directly after each other, and Petrarch sees his own life fly past in a moment. He sees Time, "the great planet", fly towards the procession of famous people. They have been famous, true enough, but the kingdoms they represent have disappeared and all honour and praise have melted like snow in the sun. Time takes all these names captive and carries them off, and people of fame must die twice – the second time wiped out by Time who triumphs over all names and the whole world. To triumph here again means "to vanquish". There is no mention of a triumphal procession in this poem. Instead we witness Time's search for, and victory over the fame that survived death. A chariot is mentioned, admittedly, but this is the traditional sun chariot, drawn by

[6] As regards the triumphs of Fame and Cupid, see C. F. Goffis, *Originalità dei " Trionfi"*, Florence, 1951.

four horses. This is a favourite motif. It has survived from the illustrations of the fall of Icarus in both literature and art. In the middle ages, the planets are described as journeying over the heavens in a chariot, but of course this is not a triumphal chariot.

Panofsky, in his article "Father Time",[7] discusses the development on this figure in the Renaissance, beginning with the illuminations of the "Triumphs"; he points out that it did not exist in antiquity and that the Renaissance in fact created this "classical" figure. He does not mention that Petrarch in his description is nearer the classical world and its use of Kronos and Saturn, when he makes the sun the personification of Time. Petrarch has chosen to describe Time primarily as a planet (the distance to Saturn is not far) and he does not make use of other attributes.

Petrarch is somewhat shaken after this confrontation with the destructiveness of Time. At the beginning of the last poem *Triumphus Eternitatis,* the triumph of eternity, he asks his heart "Whom do you believe in?" and it answers "In God who has never forsaken those who believe in Him, whereas the world and Time have brought disappointment". While his thoughts are centred in this idea, a new world appears before him, immovable and eternal. The sun, the heavens and the stars seem more beautiful and happier. In this new world Time has been stopped. Concepts such as past, present and future exist no more. He is confronting "il sommo bene" (the highest good, or paradise). Heavenly bodies that measure out life and death with their passage have no place here. Those who sing in the highest choir will be remembered throughout eternity. Time is dead, the years will no longer have control over human fame. Here Petrarch finds Laura again and many faces, unrecognizable in their suffering while under Cupid's or Time's domination, now become beautiful again. However this state of grace is but a vision and when it will be realized he does not know. It will be part of a Resurrection and a Judgement Day, where everyone is given a fair trial and where Time and Death, the conquerors of Earth, lose their power so that genuine fame is once more allowed to exist. While the first five triumphs took place on Earth, the final one takes place in Heaven. Here Petrarch will see Laura again. If it was a delight for him to see her on earth how much more will it please him to see her in heaven: "se fu beato chi la vide in terra, or che fia dunque a rivederla in cielo?" This is the triumph that shows least similarity with a classical triumph. There is no mention of any battle, procession, or laying of a triumphal wreath, but the de-

---

[7] E. Panofsky, "Father Time", in *Studies in Iconology,* cit. pp. 69-93.

scription of a state which can be created only by a just God, whom Petrarch names at the start of the poem. Thus he approaches the idea of Ecclesia triumphans which together with the Ecclesia militans, was a well-known one in the Middle Ages. Several paintings from this period can be said to correspond to the state Petrarch describes, although no close connection can be traced. In the Church of Santa Maria Novella in Florence there is a representation of the Apotheosis of Thomas Aquinas (Fig. 7) where he is surrounded by the various theological virtues. There is in the same chapel a representation of how the Dominicans help people to find heaven, (Fig. 8) a heaven where everyone is once more beautiful, as is the case in Petrarch's vision, and where "il sommo coro" (the highest choir) sings for God. There is more connection between Petrarch's vision and these pictures than there is with the Judgement Day pictures of the time. Petrarch has completely avoided any vision of Hell. His mortal sufferings in the form of his earthly love for Laura are in themselves a sort of Hell and the happiness he will experience in her company in heaven will be his paradise. One can see from this, that his love for Laura is a real, human one, and not like Dante's for Beatrice, purely spiritual.

While Dante's graphic descriptions of Hell, Purgatory and Paradise did inspire artists of his own time to illustrate them – although they generally omitted the Paradise[8] – the first known illustrations of the Triumphs are from the fifteenth century. The Latin titles may have daunted the medieval artist, or, rather, they were without meaning to him. Adolfo Venturi, in his work on the Triumphs, notes that usually literature precedes painting as regards motifs.[9] It is a fact that classical motifs did not really enter painting before the middle of the fifteenth century. But from then on we find many illustrations of the Triumphs, the most popular work of Petrarch at that time, as it pleased both his Latin and his Italian readers.[10] The whole included visions, allegories and historical, mythological and religious elementes and thus gave plenty of scope for artists. But, it must be added here, in examining Petrarch's significance for art in the fifteenth century, the surprising fact is that his subject matter is used in an almost stereotyped fashion, interpreted in a way for which the poems give no basis. There always existed a certain tendency to the stereotyped, since

---

[7] E. Panofsky, "Father Time", *Studies in Iconology,* cit. pp. 69-93.

[8] On Dante illustrations see "Dante e l'arte figurativa" of Ferruccio Ulivo, in *Dante,* ed. Umberto Parrichi, Rome, 1965.

[9] Adolfo Venturi, "Les Triomphes de Petrarque dans l'art représentatif", in *Revue de l'art ancien et moderne,* Vol. 20, 1906, pp. 81-93 and 209-221.

[10] See Walter Binni, *I classici italiani nella storia delle critica.* I, Firenze, 1956. p. 102.

Fig. 7. Andrea da Firenze, the Triumph of the Dominicans, Cappellone degli Spagnuoli, Santa Maria Novella, Florence.

Fig. 8. Andrea de Firenze, the Activity of the Domenicans, Cappella degli Spagnuoli, Santa Maria Novella, Florence.

the illustrators were more or less copying each other – as we can see in the illustrations of the Divine Comedy – but usually the illustrations did follow the text.

We have illustrations in manuscripts, either as miniatures or in woodcuts, and we find motifs from Petrarch' triumphs on bridal kists (cassoni), as complete paintings, as tapestries, stained glass, on china and glass, and a few examples of reliefs on ivory, bronze and marble. The earliest painting on a chest is from 1414 by the Sienese artist, Andrea Vanni. For chest paintings, the first two triumphs, the Triumph of Love and the Triumph of Virtue, were usually chosen, though there are examples of the others used. This is true of Pesellino of Florence, a well known cassone-painter from the first half of the fifteenth century. The Triumph of Love was also used to decorate the trays on which gifts were borne in to a woman, directly after childbirth (deschi da parto). Here is the first sign that it was the title rather than the poet's message that had captivated the artist and his public. The tragic story of the cruel Cupid and his victims was hardly a subject for a woman lying in childbed!

There is no preserved representation of all Petrarch's triumphs as a continuous whole with figures appearing in more than one triumph as is the case in the poem. Mantegna, it is known, painted the six scenes in 1501, as part of the decoration for the theatre for the Duke of Mantova. But a copy of these seems to show that Mantegna, like other painters, kept the six Triumphs separated in six clear scenes.[11] A ceiling painting by Girolamo Mocetto about 1500[12] has the Triumph of Cupid and the Triumph of Fame along with two classical triumphs in an encyclopaedic decoration, also including Roman and Biblical heroes, Virtues and Muses. In other words by this time it has been absorbed into the Renaissance world's picture gallery of accepted knowledge.

The many artists who illustrated Petrarch's manuscripts drew most inspiration from the poem. We have many illustrations and they are of a very high quality. Those shown here come from a Florentine manuscript from just before the middle of the fifteenth century. There are, as mentioned, no illustrated manuscripts preserved of this work from the fourteenth century, and whether any existed is not certain. One does not have to look at more than a few examples of the "trionfi" illustrations before one realizes that they are rather uniform in appearance. All the triumphs are depicted as classical triumphal processions with a figure sitting in a chariot drawn by animals or human beings, and surrounded by a crowd of people, even if Petrarch only

---

[11] They are now found in Washington.
[12] They are now found in Mus. Jacquemart-André, Paris.

Fig. 9. The Triumph of Cupid. Miniature from a Florentine Manuscript of the first half of the fifteenth century. Biblioteca Nazionale, Florence.

Fig. 10. The Triumph of Chastity. Biblioteca Nazionale, Florence.

Fig. 11. The Triumph of Death. Biblioteca Nazionale, Florence.

used this arrangement in the Triumph of Cupid (Fig. 9). His chariot is drawn by white horses, but in the illustrations these are occasionally replaced by oxen, tortoises or mermaids, all chosen for their symbolic associations. Cupid is often blindfolded or appears with a torch in his hand. The blindfolded Cupid is a medieval creation[13], while his torch is classical, Castita (Fig. 10), not represented at all by Petrarch, is introduced enthroned in a chariot, drawn by two unicorns, symbols of purity. Death (Fig. 11), depicted as a skeleton, with scythe and hour-glass, drives over the dead in his chariot drawn by black oxen or buffaloes. Fame, not described by Petrarch, becomes, at the hand of the artists illustrating his manuscripts, a female figure bearing a trumpet and riding in a chariot drawn by elephants.[14] Time is often depicted in a way which resembles Petrarch's own description more closely. He is the sun, in a chariot drawn by deer to symbolize swiftness. The Triumph of Eternity (Fig. 12) differs from the others in that the symbol of the Trinity is drawn on a chariot by the

[13] E. Panofsky, op. cit. "Blind Cupid", p. 95. In *Il Canzoniere*, CXVII, Petrarch describes Cupid as follows: "cieco non già ma faretrato il veggio" (not blind but with arrows), here just as in Triumphus Cupidnis he makes it clear, that he is aware of one tradition but chooses another, the classical one.

[14] Like Pompey's triumphal chariot, according to Pliny's description.

Fig. 12. The Triumph of Eternity. Biblioteca Nazionale, Florence.

four Evangelists. This pattern repeats itself with surprising regularity in all Petrarch manuscripts. The first printed and illustrated edition appeared in Venice in 1488. The illustrations are woodcuts (Figs. 13-14). Other versions follow but they are less interesting. Incidentally it is worth noting that the new interest in Petrarch evident in literature after Bembo published *Il Canzoniere* in 1501, was not followed by a corresponding interest in art. Dante, on the other hand, now became a popular pictorial subject, and now all parts of his poem are illustrated. In the sixteenth century there is very little art in Italy directly inspired by Petrarch's works. In France, Germany and Flanders, however, illustrations in books, tapestries and stained glass show evidence of Petrarch's influence, though nothing here is of the same quality as in the Italian productions.

The first to point out the uniformity which has characterised two centuries of illustrations of Petrarch's Triumphs throughout Europe, was Eugène Müntz, the author of the only book about these illustations to date.[15] He suggests that there once existed an early edition of the Triumphs, which through an accompanying commentary created the iconography. This theory is dis-

[15] Victor d' Essling and Eugêne Müntz, *Petrarque: ses études d'art, son influence sur les artistes, ses portraits et ceux de Laura, les illustrations de ses écrits*, Paris, 1902.

Fig. 13. The Triumph of Time. Woodcut, Venice, 1488. Biblioteca Vittorio Emmanuele, Rome.

Fig. 14. The Triumph of Chastity. Biblioteca Nazionale, Florence.

missed by Werner Weisbach,[16] who thins that the explanation lies in the contemporary interest in festive processions. With the rise of humanism and the resulting interest in all things classical, the Roman triumphal procession was also revived in Italy in its original form as a festive procession after a successful battle.[17] At the same time triumphal processions of Roman Emperors were "presented" as theatrical pieces, based on descriptions from antiquity. The triumphal march is, all in all, characteristic of Renaissance festivities, and the concept covers a wide range of religious or secular subjects. It is Weisbach's belief that a group of people responsible for such a festivity chose to "present" Petrarch's triumphs so that even the more abstract aspects had to be given human form. It is from these presentations that the first illustrators and bridal kist decorators drew their inspiration. He feels that the fact that many of the same "stage-properties" appear in several different illustrations, while the people are different, supports his theory. It could gain further support from the fact that the chariot of Eternity, representing a religious concept, was drawn by people. Florence seems to have been the first place where such a procession was held. Weisbach does not think that the illustrations could have inspired the processions, which is Müntz's suggestion. This is because several details seem to have been chosen as part of a festivity: for example the towering super-structures on some of the chariots designed for a number of people.

It is difficult to agree with either Müntz or Weisbach. First of all, if one studies the many illustrations very attentively, they are less uniform than they appear to Müntz and Weisbach: the animals are not the same, the figures are different and also their attributes. Only the chariots and the crowds are never missing. But it is very unlikely that there is only one explanation for this iconography.[18] Müntz's theory is shaky: so little of what he says can be proved. Perhaps some parts of Weisbach's theory are correct. It is possible that the presentation of classical triumphal processions in Florence – and he emphasizes

---

[16] Werner Weisbach, "Petrarca und die Bildende Kunst", in *Repertorium für Kunstwissenschaft*, XXVI, 1903-04, pp. 226-87.

[17] They are first known from Naples, where King Alfonso held a triumphal procession in 1443, immortalized with a triumphal arch. In 1453, Duke Borso d'Este marched in triumphal procession into Reggio which he had been given without battle by the emperor, Frederik III. Federico di Urbino marched into Florence in 1472 after having conquered Volterra. Pope Julius, in 1506, made his entry into Bologna "like a new Caesar". See W. Weisbach, *Trionfi*, Berlin, 1919.

[18] G. Caradente, in *I trionfi del primo Rinascimento*, Torino, 1963, and E. Gombrich, in "Apollonio di Giovanni" in *The Journal of the Warburg and Courtauld Institutes*, 1955, 1-2, treat some cassone masters who have a tradition of their own.

Florence as originator and standard setter – was the source of inspiration for the chariot processions. But there were no unicorns, elephants or deer in such a procession. So obviously some of the inspiration came from literature, either classical literature – there we can find that Pompey used elephants in his triumphal march – or medieval mythology and books of symbols which Petrarch also used.[19] It has already been said that some of the symbols and attributes are classical creations of Renaissance art. Obviously the illustrators had never read Petrarch's work, or else they, and their public in the fifteenth century find what they want to find in the Triumphs. When the afore-mentioned revival of interest in Petrarch's works develops in Italy in the sixteenth century, while the illustrations are becoming fewer in the same period, one finds, on the other hand, that great artists there give an entirely different interpretation of Petrarch's Triumphs, much more in keeping with the spirit of the work, while artists in other countries, especially those responsible for the French tapestries of this period, keep to the old system.

Piero della Francesca is an example of an artist from the fifteenth century who has gained a different kind of inspiration from Petrarch's work than the illustrators had. He depicts the Duke and Duchess of Urbino each seated in a triumphal chariot; the Duchess is portrayed as Virtue herself, in the same way as Laura is, and her chariot is drawn by unicorns, while the Duke, as a conqueror in triumph, is less reminiscent of Petrarch (Figs. 15-16).

One has to be careful about attributing all the triumphs that appeared in the fifteenth century as paintings or murals, to the inspiration of Petrarch. There was a general interest in this subject at the time. But in some cases the inspiration can have come only from Petrarch. For example many artists, amongst them Perugino, Mantegna and Signorelli, have found inspiration in his description of the battle between Cupid and Venus Pudicitia (Fig. 17).

To the question put forward by Müntz: why is the triumph iconography so stereotyped, a single answer will probably never be found. The question loses some of its force when a wider investigation shows, as mentioned before, that the stereotypes are less pronounced than Müntz and Weisbach claim. But another question can be posed: why do there exist such discrepancies between Petrarch's descriptions in the triumphs and the illustrations of the poems? The answer to this question is important if one wishes to clarify Petrarch's relationship to the Middle Ages and the Renaissance. In other cases where his poems

---

[19] For example, Fulgentius from about the sixth century and Albricus from the twelfth century. See J. Seznec, op. cit. p. 173.

Fig. 15. Piero della Francesca: The Triumph of Battista Sforza, Uffizi, Florence.

Fig. 16. Piero della Francesca: The Triumph of Federico II da Montefeltro, Uffizi, Florence.

Fig. 17. Luca Signorelli: The Triumph of Chastity, National Gallery, London.

have been illustrated, these differences are not found. *De Viris Illustribus* for example, and *Africa,* both written in Latin with themes based on Roman history, have illustrations in the classical spirit of the texts. The discrepancies in the Triumphs may arise from Petrarch's use of Latin titles which suggest a series of triumphal processions according to a classical model, with philosophical and moral concepts in all the roles. If one does not read the poems, or reads only the first, one may well create some of the features that are found. The fact that the first illustrations belong to the fifteenth century, when the Renaissance was well on the way, gives further evidence in favour of the view artists were captivated by the classical elements in the Triumphs; it has already been mentioned that this could not have been the case in the fourteenth century. The artists of the Renaissance disregarded the fact that some of the triumphs are medieval allegories or glorifications of the type found in contemporary religious paintings,[20] or that like other medieval poets, for example Dante, Petrarch was happy to let Roman emperors walk side by side with Old Testament characters and those of more recent times. The artists availed themselves of the elements they could use and felt they were under no obligation to keep to the text. They illustrated the poem with pictures, whose details were common to Renaissance art, even if some of them – as the blindfolded Cupid mentioned above – were creations of the Middle Ages. They made their own picture poems out of Petrarch's titles, none of them saw that Petrarch had written only one Triumph, Laura's triumph; or they needed an illustration for every poem and could not make only one triumphal procession, when Petrarch had mentioned six.

All the complications that have arisen have done so because Petrarch himself did not feel bound to either the classical or the medieval world but moved freely backwards and forwards between them. The artists who came after him saw only his connections with the classical world and therefore labelled him a Renaissance writer. But his imagery in the Triumphs proves that this is not the case. If he had been a Renaissance writer his imagery would have corresponded to content. In art history Fritz Saxl and Erwin Panofsky were amongst the first to establish that only when a classical model is matched by classical subject-matter, do we have a genuine Renaissance. Applying this to literature we will see that although Petrarch was the first to use the expression "the dark ages" of the period after the fall of the Roman Empire,[21] this does not necessarily mean that he belonged to the Renaissance. He was inconsequential in his attitude to antiquity and his historical works in Latin alone cannot make him into a Renaissance writer; nowhere so much as in the Triumphs does he demonstrate that he belongs to the Middle Ages, but to that part of it where there existed a living sense for the classical tradition.

These free connections to two worlds that we found in the Triumphs can be seen also in Petrarch's interest in art. Pictures had a great importance for him. This can be seen in his friendship with Simone Martini and the way he took care of the illustrations he made for him. It can be seen also in the high estimation he had of the painting of Giotto that he owned. These two artists are very

---

[20] Compare the afore-mentioned triumph of St Thomas Aquinas in S. Maria Novella in Florence. In this connection, the triumph of St Francis in the church of Assisi may also be mentioned.
    [21] See T.E. Mommsen, "Petrarch on the 'Dark Ages'", in *Medieval and Ranaissance Studies*, Ithaca, N.Y. 1959.

different, especially in their relations to classical art; Simone Martini moves inside the world of the Middle Ages, using only its own language, while Giotto in his pictures uses forms and stylistic elements which had their roots in antiquity. Some of his motifs he has also found there, as the afore-mentioned chariot, used by Elijah and St Francis. We will never hear Petrarch saying that he prefers one of them to the other. In the Triumphs we found inspiration from Giotto's chariot in the car of Cupid, and in the Triumph of Death Petrarch and Laura are sitting conversing under some trees, like Vergil in the illumination of Simone Martini. Other artists of his time were important to him, for example, as has already been mentioned, Petrarch may have taken the wings of a thousand colours from Cavallino, an artist belonging to the last generation of Roman–Byzantine painters. Consequently we can see that Petrarch did not exclusively seek his inspiration in the work of artists of classical tendencies, or from the art and literature of antiquity. Twice in the Triumphs he shows clearly that he departs from a tradition: first, in his description of Cupid, differing from the medieval one, second, when, after having referred to classical writers, he prefers not to give any external personification at all to Fame. But the freedom that he felt to use or ignore the classical models, was not felt by his illustrators, so they put in the classical elements omitted by Petrarch, and if posterity interprets Petrarch primarily as a classical poet, a great deal of the responsibility is theirs.

Odense University

Pictorial illustration of late medieval poetic texts: the role of the frontispiece or prefatory picture

by Elizabeth Salter and Derek Pearsall

The object of this paper is to examine some of the ways in which medieval pictures may help us in the understanding and interpretation of medieval works of literature, specifically medieval narratives. There are a number of ways in which this subject has been tackled in the past, and some of these may usefully be identified at the outset, so that what we are trying to do can be seen in perspective. Three modes of approach may be mentioned that have proved influential.

1. Stylistic

This approach assumes that all the arts will be responsive, in terms of their own medium, to certain common cultural influences at a particular period, and that they can be investigated therefore as elements in a general cultural pattern. Wylie Sypher, for instance, in his *Four Stages of Renaissance Style* (1955), which in its turn is heavily indebted to H. Wölfflin, *Principles of Art History* (1915), sees the achievement of what he calls 'Renaissance style' as the integration of fragmentary Gothic naturalism into a unified composition, done according to a fixed point of view and according to established principles of compositional harmony. Gothic, by contrast, is fraught with peril and duality, restless, strained; it holds a perilous equilibrium of contrary forces; its essential structure is sequential and successive rather than compositional. You move through an illuminated page, where you take in a Renaissance painting; you walk round a Gothic cathedral, where you look for the right vantage point from which to see a baroque building. Likewise, as Sypher says, *Troilus* is an experience in linearity; the contrary pressures of human experience and transcendental significance create a precarious balance; the world in which the characters live is strongly suggestive of reality but only partly organised, like Giotto's (Sypher, p. 69). Such views are very stimulating, but it will be seen that the terms of reference are too broad to allow much more than the suggestion of interesting perspectives. The tendency is towards an increasing abstraction, towards a vague half-world where shadowy essences like 'realism' and 'unity of composition' cry out for reincarnation in the specificity of their own medium. At worst, it all descends into mere impressionism, a guessing game where painters and writers have to be matched in appropriate pairs – Botticelli and Spenser, El Greco and Donne, Rubens and Milton.

2. Iconographic

This approach is fundamentally different, since it assumes that what picture and text have in common is the expression of a like content. In the work of D. W. Robertson, for instance, particularly *A Preface to Chaucer* (1962), picture and text are submitted to an ideological screening in which only those meanings are allowed to come through which conform to orthodox Christian doctrine. Considerations of style, of artistic individuality, of genre, of historical context, of particularity in the relation of content and form, are relegated, as being of lesser importance, or else are neglected completely. In this kind of interpretation, the picture, like the literary text, is an encoded message; both are read, and can only be read, by the application of a code provided by iconographic and allegorical techniques, and the test of the validity of the code is that it should always produce the same kinds of meaning. It must be acknowledged that the isolation of precise iconographic motifs is an important achievement of Robertson's kind of analysis, and that his use of pictures can be an effective and proper means of reinforcing his arguments. His accounts of the iconography of the shrew, of the bagpipes, of the cock and fox, for instance, have an important bearing on our reading of various of the *Canterbury Tales,* especially where he is recovering for us something of the pictorial experience of the medieval writer. But this is not of course the limit of Robertson's claims for his method, and those larger claims must be sceptically regarded.

3. Structural

Structural analogies between pictures and literary texts are frequently made on general stylistic grounds, as in the book by Sypher. But a characteristic mode of interpretation adopted by a good deal of modern Chaucer criticism treats structural analogy as a key to underlying ideological unity. The clues are again given by Robertson, as in his account of *The House of Fame:*

> In *The House of Fame* the various parts all concern the same speaker, and they appear in narrative sequence, but otherwise they have little outward connection with one another. We may compare this situation with the arrangement of the pages in one of the great East Anglian psalters, where

there is no explicit relationship between the marginalia and the initials (*A Preface to Chaucer*, p. 284).

The direction of the argument is clear: if Chaucer's narratives lack organic unity in the same way that Beatus pages lack compositional unity, then both must possess some other kind of unity, that is, inorganic unity, unity which is derived from the reference of the aggregated parts of the composition to an external unity, that of Christian doctrine. R. M. Jordan's book, *Chaucer and the Shape of Creation* (1967), which is subtitled *The Aesthetic Possibilities of Inorganic Structure*, extends this argument, seeking structural analogies for literature primarily in architecture, which in its turn is analysed in terms of its use of mathematical and musical symbolism. A poem is to be thought of as "an edifice composed of prefabricated parts" (p. 43), and there is much talk of the effects achieved through the aggregation of discrete units, and much fanciful analogy, as between the exposed jointing of Gothic building and the explicit transitions of medieval narrative. At one point, we find Jordan saying:

> The reader can move among the finely fashioned parts of *Troilus* much as he can move within a Gothic cathedral, admiring the parts individually and admiring the capacity for order which unites them into an ordered, aggregative whole (p. 91).

The bemused reader may think there is no possible way in which reading the *Troilus* is like walking round a Gothic cathedral, and there is an example here of the way in which a sophisticated and well-developed taste for abstraction can in the end eliminate the object from view altogether. Jordan's tastes in this direction can be well seen in that there are only three illustrations in his book: two of those are plans of churches and one is a diagram of the geocentric universe.

One could go further, and say that the defect of all the approaches to the relationship of literary text and picture we have been discussing is the tendency towards abstraction. Certain features of a work of art are selected, extracted from their context and described in abstract language; a similar set of features, derived from another work of art in the same way and clothed in the same kind of language, is matched with them, and a cry of delight greets the startling similarity that is revealed. Philosophically, it could be called the search for unity in diversity; from another point of view, it is a word-game.

It would seem, therefore, that attention to the relationships between pictures and literary texts should respect the integrity and essential uniqueness of each, and recognise the importance too of individual cultural context and function. It is possible to do this, in a properly scrupulous way, when examining those literary texts where the literary inspiration is derived from pictorial models, where the writer, that is, is thinking of pictures; or when examining the treatment of common subject-matter, such as portraiture or landscape. But one of the most tempting fields of study is that in which the artist is working directly under the influence of a literary text, especially a contemporary literary text. Here, we may feel, we may gain some insight into a culturally relevant understanding of a work of literature such as we rarely have access to. Literary criticism in the Middle Ages is a highly developed art, but it has almost nothing to do with the vernacular literature actually being produced, and like all literary criticism it is to some extent imprisoned within its own conceptual vocabulary. But an artist, even if his pictorial vocabulary has to be recovered by historical study, will surely offer us an immediacy of imaginative response to the significance of a literary text which will enhance our understanding in a unique way.

Such may be the case with some great book-illustrators, such as Dickens' Boz, but unfortunately it is not often the case with the illustration of medieval secular narratives, which is the subject of immediate concern here. The illustration of the medieval French *Lancelot,* for instance, as Alison Stones has shown, is mostly done by the lesser artists of the *atelier,* and usually draws upon a repertoire of stock motifs which are applied, more or less indiscriminately, to the narrative.[1] Scenes of mêlée, of siege, of meeting and departure, of procession, of court ceremonial, are dotted about the manuscripts, more, it seems, with the intention of providing visual relief and variety, or of punctuating the narrative in a visually convenient way, than of providing a visual commentary on or interpretation of the narrative. Occasionally, as we see in Margaret Manion's analysis of the Melbourne copy of a French *Livy,* the artist will pick up for illustration some stray incident of no more than peripheral importance.[2] This does at least indicate that someone has read the text, probably the workshop supervisor, but in this case only with an eye for the illustratable scene, not for the scene that is particularly significant in narrative

---

[1] See esp. M. Alison Stones, "Secular Manuscript Illumination in France", in *Medieval Manuscripts and Textual Criticism* (1976), pp. 83-102.

[2] In her lecture, "Illustrated history in contemporary guise, with specific reference to the Melbourne Livy", given at the Seminar on *The Waning of the Middle Ages* at the Humanities Research Centre of the Australian National University at Canberra, August, 1978.

terms. Such scenes are often chosen because they provide opportunities for the employment of traditional iconographical models from the illustration of religious MSS: it is not that any underlying religious significance is being brought out, but that the availability of appropriate compositional models is an important consideration for the professional illustrator.[3] The *Roman de la Rose* is another extensively illustrated secular narrative, but again the interpretation of the narrative offered by the illustrations is not particularly illuminating. There is usually a heavy concentration of illustrative matter in the scenes portraying the figures painted on the outside of the garden-wall, such as Avarice, Wrath, Old Age, Poverty and Envy, and the illustrative programme tends to be sparse after that. But this is for pragmatic reasons: (i) illustration always tends to be heavier in the earlier part of a manuscript; (ii) the scenes are themselves paintings, and therefore apt for illustration; (iii) models are readily available in the portrayal of the Deadly Sins in *Somme le Roi* and other manuscripts. For this reason, amongst others, Fleming's attempt to press the pictures into the service of an ideological interpretation of the *Roman*[4] is unconvincing and involves a good deal of speculation and wilful neglect of context and workshop practice. Much more interesting is the work of Rosemond Tuve on fifteenth-century illustrations of the *Roman* (as well as Deguileville and Christine de Pisan) in her book *Allegorical Imagery* (1966). What she does throws no light on the interpretation of the poem in terms of the purposes of the original composition, but she is able to illustrate certain changes in the reception of the poem, particularly of its allegory, by studying changes in illustrative technique. Some shift towards the literalisation of conceptual allegorical images is certainly detectable in the examples she proffers.

    Illustration of English secular narrative texts, of course, lags a long way behind continental practice, and it is not until the fifteenth century that we get extended programmes of illustration for works like Gower's *Confessio Amantis,* or Lydgate's *Troy-Book* and *Fall of Princes.* These constitute a study in themselves, which has not yet been done. For the rest, there are only the little miniatures of the Auchinleck MS, most of them now lost; the coarse illustrations of *Gawain and the Geen Knight* and the other poems of MS Cotton Nero A.X; the crude cycle attached to the Bodley 264 text of *Alexander and Dindimus;* and the very sparse programme offered in early MSS of the *Confessio Amantis,* usually consisting of just two pictures, the statue of Nebuchadnezzar's dream

---

[3] See e.g. H. Buchthal, *Historia Troiana: Studies in the History of Medieval Secular Illustration* (London, 1971).

[4] J. V. Fleming, *The Roman de la Rose: a Study in Allegory and Iconography* (Princeton, 1969).

and the lover confessing to Genius. The former is very interesting, especially if it was done at Gower's instigation – a very rare occurrence indeed in the study of illustrated manuscripts – since it could contribute to a significant reshaping of our view of the poem and especially of the importance of its didactic framework.

The great gap in the period is of course the absence of any extensively illustrated Chaucer MSS. The few that exist are interesting, but they could rarely be said to contribute significantly to our understanding of Chaucer's poetry. The most famous is the Ellesmere MS of the *Canterbury Tales,* which includes portraits of the pilgrims on horseback set in the MS without frame at the point where the pilgrim begins his tale. The portraits are done with an unusual degree of fidelity to the detail of the text, though not with complete fidelity, and we are clearly dealing with a careful and deliberate attempt to underline the meaning of the poem and enhance its appeal. It is true that the portraits have their own stylistic and iconographical models, and in some cases these models dominate the composition, sometimes aptly, as in the rendering of the Squire as a stereotype of the 'month of May' in the Calendar series of the Books of Hours; sometimes inaptly, as in the rendering of the Doctor of Physic as the satirical stereotype of the physician inspecting urine-samples. But the artist, or the supervisor who gave him his instructions, shows himself responsive to the concrete and detailed texture of Chaucer's realism, and there is no systematic tendency for the portraits to fall back completely into pictorial stereotype – which is the development we might have expected. Furthermore, the placing of the portraits at the appropriate points in the *Tales,* and not beside the portraits of the pilgrims in the General Prologue, shows a recognition of the dramatic structure of the *Canterbury Tales,* as a whole. We often tend to think that the development of the idea of the 'dramatic principle' in the *Canterbury Tales* has been the work of modern critics such as Kittredge and Lumiansky. But clearly here, within a year or two of Chaucer's death, the importance of the dramatic principle, of the existence of the Tales as narrations by dramatically conceived characters, was very fully recognised, and reinforced as an interesting and attractive feature of the poem's composition. Indeed, the provision of the pictures is only one of several moves in this direction for which the Ellesmere supervisor may be responsible.

Beyond that, there is very little. Cambridge University Library MS Gg. 4.27 once had its own cycle of pilgrim portraits, but few remain, and the illustration of the MS is dominated by the portraits of the sins in the *Parson's Tale,* which clearly represent a recourse to traditional models, and are of little interest for our understanding of the *Parson's Tale* – not that it is a tale which needs much understanding. There are a few little initial minatures for *Canterbury Tales* MSS, of no more than passing interest,[5] and the miniature for *The Complaint of Mars* in Bodley MS Fairfax 16, which may be of some limited significance. We have to remember, in our search for the 'literary' significance of pictures, that illustrations are introduced into manuscripts of secular literature for a wide variety of reasons, many of them 'non-literary'. They may be in the nature of a compliment to the distinguished patrons, for whom the book was intended: pictures in manuscripts of Christine de Pisan's poems, for instance, presented to the royal house of France, or in manuscripts commissioned by or given to Jean, duc de Berry, serve first of all as a statement of the importance of the status of the recipient and of the ceremonial significance of the making and the delivering of the book.[6] Illustrations may be introduced for commercial and pragmatic reasons: illustrations improve saleability in certain markets by enhancing the prestige and increasing the cost of a manuscript, while for the reader they provide a resting point for the eye, or a pleasant substitute for reading the text. In such practical circumstances, we could even say that it is the boring poems that most need illustration, whilst the interesting ones will look after themselves. So we cannot, initially, expect too much of our Chaucer manuscripts.

On the other hand, we might have expected more of our *Troilus* manuscripts. What a poem to illustrate, one might think. A *frisson* ran round the scholarly world when the 3rd revised edition of Derek Brewer's book on *Chaucer* came out in 1973 complete with a cycle of illustrations to accompany the discussion of *Troilus and Criseyde*. Some of the interest subsided when the small print revealed that the pictures were taken from a late 15th century manuscript of the French *Roman de Troyle et Criseide*, but the event only emphasised again the gap in the evidence from England. Even the manuscript presented to the future Henry V, while still Prince of Wales, the Campsall MS (Pierpont Morgan Library MS 817), though nicely written, has only one historiated initial, some illuminated border-work and pen flourishes. However, there is one illustration in a *Troilus* MS which deserves our concentrated attention, both for what it reveals and for what it has been said to reveal. This

---

[5] For a full account of the illustrations in MSS of the *Canterbury Tales* see the chapter by Margaret Rickert, "Illumination", in *The Text of the Canterbury Tales,* ed. J. M. Manly and Edith Rickert, 8 vols. (Chicago, 1940), vol. 1, pp. 561-605.

[6] See, for instance, British Library MS Harley 4431, *Poésies* of Christine de Pisan, presented to Isabeau de Bavière, and Vienna MS 2537, a prose *Tristan* owned by Jean de Berry.

Corpus Christi College Cambridge MS 61. Chaucer, *Troilus and Criseyde*

is the frontispiece to Corpus Christi College Cambridge MS 61, the only survivor of a programme of illustration for which 90 blank spaces remain as evidence, and one of the most splendid examples of fifteenth century English bookpainting. The picture has proved enigmatic for art-historians, because of its uniqueness and the multiplicity of models upon which it draws, but it has been an irresistible temptation to literary critics.[7] Margaret Galway is not the only one who has seen in the picture a representation of an actual historical event – Chaucer reading his poem to the assembled court at an outdoor occasion at Wallingford castle in 1385. Not everyone goes as far as Galway in identifying all the personages represented, but the general acceptance of her view is well demonstrated in the way the picture is conventionally referred to as 'Chaucer reading to the court of Richard II'. No book, as will be seen, is in evidence. Furthermore, no art-historian would countenance for a moment the identification of all the minor personnel of a picture when there are no specific identifying features such as coats of arms, insignia or characteristic costume. The speculations that have been attached to the miniature are a good example of the neglect by literary scholars of matters of art-historical context that are essential to the interpretation of pictures, and it would have been well if they had taken more sober note of the early comment by the art-historian, Eric Millar:

> cette miniature ne laisse pas que d'être énigmatique. . . elle occupe une place à part dans l'histoire de l'art anglais...[8]

The standard interpretation of the frontispiece as an authentic record or reconstruction of the original manner of 'publication' of Chaucer's poem has had important consequences, for the evidence it provides has been allowed to stand as historical and objective substantiation of a view of Chaucer as 'a poet of the Court' for which other evidence is fragmentary and partial. The fact that it may have been for this very reason that the picture was introduced in the first place makes no great difference to our view of its reliability. If, for instance, the volume was a commercial venture, it may have been very much in the interests of its producer to make the claim that Caucer was granted the

---

[7] For discussion of the picture, with full references, see D. Pearsall, "The *Troilus* Frontispiece and Chaucer's Audience", *Yearbook of English Studies* 7 (1977), 68-74; *Troilus and Criseyde,* a facsimile of Corpus Christi College Cambridge MS 61, with Introductions by M. B. Parkes and Elizabeth Salter (D. S. Brewer: Cambridge, 1978), esp. pp. 15-23.

[8] *La Miniature Anglaise* (Paris et Bruxelles, 1928), pp. 44-5.

Pierpont Morgan Library, New York, MS 772. Deguileville, *Pelerinage de la vie Humaine*

very highest kind of royal and aristocratic patronage. If, however, we take note of the anticipated lavishness of its illustration, and the unusually fine nature of its script, and hold that it was too expensive a project to be anything but a response to patronage, we must still be extremely careful about the way in which we use the frontispiece as a witness to historical truth. That Chaucer was a poet of the court, in the sense of the inner royal and autocratic circle, may be true or untrue; the frontispiece can provide only ambiguous support for whichever theory we may wish to advance.[9]

In pursuing the enigma of the *Troilus* frontispiece, the present authors have attempted in the essays cited above (note 7) to demonstrate iconographic models for the lower register of the frontispiece in standard preaching pictures of the fourteenth and fifteenth centuries. These pictures are found in a variety of manuscript (and panel) contexts, and can be shown to work a number of variations upon a well-established iconographical format. Most significantly for our present purposes, they are found as frontispiece or prefatory author-

[9] For various positions in the debate, see D. Pearsall, *Old English and Middle English Poetry* (Routledge: London, 1977), pp. 189-97; E. Salter, "Chaucer and Internationalism", *Studies in the Age of Chaucer* 2 (1980), 71-9.

Bibliothèque Nationale, Paris, MS f.fr. 376. Deguileville, *Pelerinage*

portraits in a number of religious texts, including the prose *Compendium super Bibliam* of Petrus de Aureolis and the first recension of the long fourteenth-century allegorical poem by Guillaume de Deguileville, *Pelerinage de la Vie Humaine*.[10] The appropriateness of such a picture to these texts is clear – especially in the case of the *Pelerinage,* which is preceded, in its first recension, by a hortatory prologue, in which the poet, who was a Cistercian monk, addresses all estates of society, rich and poor, kings and queens, pilgrims, fools and wise men.[11] The appropriateness of the picture to Chaucer's *Troilus* is a more complex matter, and will be discussed in greater detail below. We may remember, however, at this stage, that the transfer of religious iconography to secular contexts is a constant activity of illuminating workships throughout the medieval period. We may also note that whoever was to have been responsible for designing the whole illustrative programme for MS Corpus 61 would have been deeply involved in finding new iconographic material; no known cycle of *Troilus* illustrations could have provided, at this early date in the fifteenth century, subjects for ninety spaces. It is not very surprising, therefore, that the frontispiece turns away from the usual kinds of author-portrait in courtly secular manuscripts – in those of Machaut, Froissart or Christine de Pisan, for instance – and exploits instead the potentialities of a religious format. That format had already shown itself to be not only highly respected in prefatory position, but also extremely attractive to a range of artists seeking variations on the theme of a mixed assembly, in outdoor or indoor settings,[12] and innovation was probably, of necessity, to be one of the key-notes of the plan for miniatures. The choice of such iconographic models by the producers of MS Corpus 61 is further evidence, of course, that they were not attempting a historically authentic reconstruction of an actual scene, nor drawing precisely upon one.

Whatever access to historical reality the picture has can only be argued on the basis of its artistic quality. The richness of its specific recall of a whole range of courtly and aristocratic illustrated manuscripts, made in French workshops between 1380 and 1415 for a number of famous continental patrons

[10] For the former, see B. L. MS Royal 8.c.iii; for the latter, Bibl. Royale (Bruxelles) MSS 10176-8 and 10197-8, Bibl. Nationale (Paris) MS f.fr.376, B. L. MS Add. 38120.

[11] Ed. J. Sturzinger (London, 1893), lines 4-6.

[12] Such scenes, of indoor and outdoor preaching, proliferate in French MSS of the fourteenth century, both religious and secular. The *Bréviaire de Belleville* and the *Heures de Jeanne de Navarre* (B. N. MSS lat. 10483-4) (Bibl. Nationale (Paris) Nouv. Acq. Lat. 3145) represent the lively series done by the Pucelle workshop for royal ladies in the second quarter of the century, while the numerous MSS of the *Chroniques de France* contain excellent examples of further elaboration towards the end of century (see essays cited in note 7 for details of MSS and some reproductions).

Bibliothèque Nationale,
Paris MS f.fr. 831
Froissart, *Poésies*

– not least of which are products of the anonymous 'Bedford Master' and the Limbourg brothers, working for Jean, Duc de Berry, in the first and second decades of the fifteenth century[13] – suggests that it cannot be isolated from the lavish courtly circumstance to which it gives expression. If we believe that the *de luxe* quality of the Corpus Christi College copy of Chaucer's poem demands our acceptance of an original patronal situation of some importance, then it is also tempting to believe that the frontispiece commemorates an early fifteenth century sense of the poet's relationship to the courtly society of the preceding century, and the prestige enjoyed by his poetry. It need not, and no doubt, does not, record a special historical moment but, in the very care which was obviously taken with its ordering and design, it may still pay tribute to a historical reputation, fostered, as we know, "this side idolatry" throughout the fifteenth century. Indeed, since analysis of the costume and style of the picture

---

[13] See Salter, Introduction to Corpus 61 facsimile, pp. 19-22.

British Library, London
MS Royal 19.c.xv
Songe du Vergier

allows us to date it no later than the first quarter of the fifteenth century,[14] we may well look for a patron among those aristocratic families who would have had the strongest reasons for preserving traditions concerning the life, both literary and official, of Geoffrey Chaucer. Such are the Montacutes, Earls of Salisbury (Alice Chaucer, granddaughter of the poet, married the fourth Earl), and the Nevilles, Dukes of Westmorland (Joan Beaufort, daughter of John of Gaunt and niece by marriage of Chaucer, was Duchess of Westmorland). The name of a later owner of the manuscript, Anne Neville, inscribed on folio 101ᵛ,[15] could take us back to the Nevilles of Westmorland (she might have been Joan Beaufort's daughter, and a distant relative, therefore, of Chaucer) or to another powerful family – the Beauchamps, Earls of Warwick: Anne Beauchamp, heiress of Richard, Earl of Warwick, married Richard Neville in

[14] Ibid., pp. 15, 21
[15] Ibid., p. 11.

Pierpont Morgan Library, New York, MS 804. Froissart, *Chroniques*

1484. All of these families are known book-owners, and some of their members are not only of discriminating taste in the collection of *de luxe* volumes, but are themselves poets and patrons of poets.[16]

Given an origin in contexts of some such character, the *Troilus* frontispiece, though most probably a fiction, would be an intelligent and sophisticated fiction – the result of informed collaborative activity between workshop, patron and received traditions. It would also in these circumstances be likely to embody an intelligent response to the text – a likelihood which can be viewed in larger European perspective, as we record the well-established convention of giving frontispiece illustration to major workshop artists, not to apprentices, and of requiring it to be based upon a thoughtful consideration of what was appropriate to the text.[17]

---

[16] John Montacute, third earl of Salisbury, executed in 1400, was a poet of international reputation and a friend of Christine de Pisan; Richard Beauchamp, earl of Warwick (d. 1439), was also a poet; Joan Beaufort, as countess of Westmoreland, was a patroness of Hoccleve; Anne Neville's name can be associated with a number of splendidly illuminated manuscripts, as can that also of Anne Beauchamp (Neville). See Pearsall, *Old English and Middle English Poetry,* pp. 194, 225, 237; Salter, Introduction, p. 23, n. 30; K. L. Scott, *The Caxton Master and his Patrons,* Cambridge Bibliographical Society, Monograph no. 8 (1976), pp. 61-2.

Bodleian Library, Oxford, MS Douce 213. Boccaccio, *Decameron*

If we now ask, more particularly, why the choice of composition was made, we find that the illustrator of such a manuscript, or the supervisor who gave him his instructions, or the patron who dealt with both, had a number of options, a number of iconographic models for frontispiece author portrayal, for example:

(1) the author as teacher, lecturing from a text book before students who follow his discourse in their own books, e.g. Azzo, author of the *Summae,* a legal

---

[17] For comment upon frontispiece composition, see M. Meiss, *French Painting in the time of Jean de Berry: The Limbourgs and their Contemporaries* (London, 1974), pp. 408-9; K. Scott, *The Caxton Master,* pp. 3-11.

text-book, in Bodl. MS Canon. misc. 416; Hugh of St Victor, in Bodl. MS Laud misc. 409.

(2) the author as writer, usually represented as writing at an upright writing desk (e.g. Macrobius, in Bodl. MS Canon. class. lat. 257) though occasionally as holding his completed book (e.g. Chaucer in B.L. MS Lansdowne 851).

(3) the author as reader, represented as reading from his book which he has before him on a lectern, e.g. Machaut, in B.N. MS f.fr. 22545; Vegetius, in Bodl. MS Laud lat. 56 (cf. also B.N. MS f.fr. 831).

(4) the author as reporter, writing as events unfold, e.g. Boccaccio (*De casibus,* French trans.) in Bodl. MS 265; Boccaccio *(Decameron),* in Bodl. MS Douce 213; Martin le Franc *(Le Champion des Dames),* in Bibl. Royale, Brussels, MS 9466.

(5) the author as preacher, e.g. as above (Note 10).

(6) the author as dreamer, e.g. Deguileville, in B.N. MS f.fr. 1647.

(7) the author as protégé of a patron, usually in the form of a presentation picture, where the author kneels before his patron holding out to him a copy of his book, e.g. *Songe du Vergier,* in Bodl. MS e Mus. 43; Pierre Salmon *(Réponses à Charles VI),* B.N. MS f.fr. 23279.

(8) the author as protagonist, represented in a famous scene from his life, e.g. Cicero *(Rhetorica ad Herennium),* in Bodl. MS Holkham 373; Petrarch *(Canzoniere),* in Bodl. MS Canon. ital. 69.

What is interesting about frontispiece illustration in the later fourteenth and fifteenth centuries is the sophistication with which it begins to work variations on these fairly simple models and the responsiveness shown to the nature of the text and its relation to its audience. In the case of the Deguileville MSS, we have interesting attempts to combine pictorial reference to the two suggestions in the text of the author's role: that the poem is a dream that he dreamt, and that the dream is valuable for others to attend to. The picture will sometimes follow the text in its order of presentation – preaching, then dreaming (Pierpont Morgan MS 772); sometimes it will rationalise this order according to natural time – dreaming, then preaching (B.N. MS fr. 376). It is worth noting, in these two pictures, the suggestion of the content of the first part of the dream in the three dimensional heavenly city shown in a mirror – a very apt iconographic choice, since the mirror was commonly used as an image of imaginative perception, and imagination was in its turn the agent of dream-experience. In another MS (B.N. MS fr. 12462) the illustrator has followed out this rationalisation into a fully literalised narrative of the events that brought

British Library, London, MS Royal 8.c.iii. Petrus de Aureolis, *Compendium Super Bibliam*

the book into being. This is evidently less apt, but clearly in the other two we have competent little summaries of the poem's action, indications of its mode of address, signposts, in a word, into the poem, which both embody and influence a response to it.

In a manuscript of the *Songe du vergier* (B.L. Roy. 19.c.xv), the combination of dreamer and dream content is extended, so as to include a quite full programmatic synopsis of the poem's action: the dreamer asleep at the bottom; above him the debate of clerk and knight which provides the body of the text; and above that, the king, flanked by spiritual and secular advisors, who is the intended recipient of the poem's instruction.

In a manuscript of Froissart's *Chroniques* (Pierpont Morgan MS 804), allusions to content are included in simultaneous combination with a presentation picture: Froissart presents his book to Richard II (this seems to conflate two books – the book of poems he presented in 1395, and the present book) while on the right Isabel, queen of Edward II, holding her young son, Edward III, by the hand, is received by Charles IV of France. Anglo-French relations are the subject of the two parts of the picture, as they are of the *Chroniques* themselves, and the whole association of picture and text hints at *entente*.

Finally, in a fifteenth century MS of Boccaccio's *Decameron* (Bodl. MS Douce 213) there is a beautifully disingenuous representation of the author as reporter, where the illusion of reportage, so assiduously cultivated by authors who are claiming, however deeply tongue-in-cheek, to be naturalistic, is represented as a living reality. Chaucer would have been delighted with such a picture for the *Canterbury Tales*.

These examples may provide a context for our return to the *Troilus* frontispiece. There are some things that the illustration could not have chosen to do: a presentation picture would have been inappropriate, given that the poem is specifically dedicated to Gower and Strode and not to any prestigious member of the nobility. But he could have chosen a simple author-as-writer scene, for instance, or author-as-reader. He chose instead a preaching scene, either adapting it himself from a plain religious setting or benefiting from some earlier adaptation, perhaps for prefatory purposes.

The reasons for doing so can only be guessed at. We have already proposed that the original conditions of the planning of the manuscript may have encouraged, even prescribed, innovation as one of the motive forces in the ordering of its illustrative programme. A combination of patronal and artistic circum-

Bibliothèque Royale, Brussels, MS 10176-8. Deguileville, *Pelerinage*

Bibliothèque Royale, Brussels, MS 10197-8. Deguileville, *Pelerinage*

stances alone may have initiated the quest for a new prefatory design.[18] The fact that Deguileville manuscripts of the *Pelerinage de la Vie Humaine,* with their preacher/poet format, and their increasingly courtly and detailed outdoor setting, were familiar in England during the early fifteenth century may be a significant factor. But they could also have been seen on the Continent by travelling members of the English upper-classes, on business of war or diplomacy. And if, as may be the case, we are dealing here with a foreign artist working in England, he could be relying upon his own memory of continental picture-models. By 1410 or 1415, wide acceptance of the literary as well as religious status of the Deguileville *Pelerinage* poems may have made the transfer of a

[18] See the early fifteenth century French document, giving a patron's directions for an elaborate prefatory picture to Sallust's *Catalina,* printed by J. Porcher, *Mélanges offerts à Franz Calot* (Paris, 1960), p. 38.

part of their special prefatory iconography to a secular work comparatively easy.[19] Kathleen Scott's study of the frontispiece to a later fifteenth century English manuscript, the Magdalene College, Cambridge, copy of Caxton's translation of the *Ovide Moralisé,* makes admirably clear the way in which artists, while working within "a tradition of author frontispieces", drew upon a variety of disparate continental models, and innovated – often by processes of transformation and fusion.[20]

There may, however, be a little more to say about the relationship of *Troilus and Criseyde* itself to the frontispiece miniature. The poem explicitly presents itself, on numerous occasions, as a performance before a live audience. The frequent references to "ye loueres that ben here", the requests to them to bring their greater understanding to bear upon what the poet does so clumsily, the comments about their reception of the story, the particular address to the women in the audience at the end of the work – all these are a profoundly important part of the poem's meaning. Chaucer's cultivation of the personality of the poet-narrator, his creation of an atmosphere of immediacy and spontaneity, as the story seems to unfold almost of its own volition – these are fundamental to his technique in the poem. Whether we think that this is simply a brilliant literary illusion, or whether we accept, rather, that the poem has multiple modes of address, some of which do refer to actual social circumstance, the *Troilus* frontispiece may stand in significant relationship to such aspects of narrational method. In one interpretation, the frontispiece can be seen only as "a product of the poem's power to create the sense of a listening group".[21] In another, it can be seen as a testimony, however, stylised and artificial in form, to a living tradition of Chaucer as "performer... to a court audience..."[22] a tradition for which the poem must allow itself to be partly responsible. Either way, the illustration is true to the work, providing an important commentary on contemporary understanding of and response to Chaucer's greatest love-poem, and intriguing us with just a suggestion that it is informed with some knowledge of Chaucer's historical rôle.

With the possibility of this kind of intelligent and sophisticated responsive-

---

[19] For early fifteenth century interest in Deguileville, see Pearsall, *OE and ME Poetry,* pp. 172-3; Salter, Introduction to Corpus 61, p. 19, n. 15.

[20] Scott, loc. cit.

[21] D. Brewer, "Troilus and Criseyde", in the Sphere *History of Literature in the English Language,* vol I: *The Middle Ages,* ed. W. F. Bolton (London, 1970), pp. 195-228 (p. 196).

[22] G. Shepherd, "Troilus and Criseyde", in *Chaucer and Chaucerians,* ed. D. Brewer (London, 1966), pp. 65-87 (p. 71).

British Library, London, MS Add. 38120. Deguileville, *Pelerinage*

Bibliothèque Nationale, Paris, MS f.fr. 22545. Machaut, *Poésies*

ness to the poem in mind, we may even turn to the upper register of the frontispiece, and recognise that it may not be merely decorative infilling. We have seen that references to the content of a literary work frequently accompany frontispiece author portrayal. The scene in the upper part of the picture may legitimately be seen as an allusion to the central event of the poem – the departure of Criseyde, amidst scenes of great courtly ceremonial, from the city of Troy. The stylistic models for the scene are principally scenes of ceremonial procession and meeting.[23] Criseyde's departure was of course a meeting too, and therein, it might be said, lies the tragic consequence of the story. In this interpretation, the frontispiece not only guides us into the poem and its modes of procedure: it also reminds us of the event which provided the germ of the whole Troilus-Criseyde story in medieval tradition, directs us beyond the present moment of beginning to consequences of the action here begun, and reinforces, amidst all the images of richness and beauty, the sad premonition of "the double sorwe of Troilus" announced by Chaucer in his opening line.

University of York

---

[23] Salter, Introduction to Corpus 61, p. 17.

Biblia Pauperum and the wall paintings in the church of Bellinge. The Book and the church wall

by KNUD BANNING

Throughout the Middle Ages the ability to read and write made a deep impression on the ordinary citizen. Where the Christian Church had been introduced the common people admired the priest who was able to produce documents concerning the properties and rights of the church, and who day after day read from his books during the Mass and other services in the church itself or in the parish.

Books and the ability to read from them were essential to the church. During his studies at the cathedral the prospective priest was taught to select the various readings according to the traditions of the diocese and to read them correctly, to chant from the antiphonary and to read from other books dealing with the ordering of church life. When he had been ordained and sent to his new parish the priest found at least some of the necessary books there, which – we suppose – were constantly being rewritten in order to bring conformity to all liturgical books within the diocese and also to introduce new trends into the liturgy. Thus the church was dependent on books and the ability to read and write. The art of printing was of course gladly accepted by the church authorities, since it made it easier for the bishop to maintain liturgical conformity, which by the end of the Middle Ages was universal. Therefore the liturgical books were often the first to be printed.

But the fascination with letters and books spread to other parts of the church as well. The Franciscan reform or revolution in the thirteenth century stressed the importance and necessity of repentence for the common man, i.e. confessing his sins to a priest or a friar, accepting forgiveness and doing penance. But the penance was not intended to consist only of special and prescribed good works. It had to come from a pious and devoted heart. This, too, was stressed by religious circles in Northern Europe, under the influence of the mysticism and the new humanistic movement from the Low Countries. In these circles books were a considerable help in the efforts to create the pious and devoted heart. Thomas à Kempis's book on the Imitation of Christ is perhaps the best known from this period, but there were many others. These books were not to be used by the clergy inside the church during the different services, but outside the church to develop private devotion. Therefore they were highly esteemed among the more prosperous citizens, who could afford to buy them. Some of these books were written by hand; later they were printed from a carved wooden log. Some of them were illustrated – a few of them in colour – but only very few survived the hazards of the following centuries. But single pages from these books are preserved, and sometimes the illustrations on them have been used as models by the painters who executed the wall-paintings in the churches.

This is the case with pages from the so-called *Biblia Pauperum,* which was highly esteemed in Central and Northern Europe. Its origin is somewhat dubious, but in this country it was used for private devotion.

Certainly nobody felt there was any discrepancy between the books that were used by the priest in front of the altar, and those intended for private devotion outside the church. But the conflict was there, and during the growth of literary humanism and the Reformation this conflict was evident. And in this church it is possible to detect some of the earlier stages of this conflict.

It must be remembered that until the twelfth and thirteenth centuries the High Altar was the natural centre in every church, and the decoration of the vaults and walls of the church was executed according to this arrangement. The head figure was the Majestas Domini in the top of the apse even in this ordinary village church. All the paintings radiated from here into the chancel and onto the chancel arch and sometimes even into the nave. The skilful painters were able to present a stable and complete universe, invisible to the naked eye outside the church, to the congregation, who both saw the history of their Saviour and His saints and found their modest place in the interminable crowd on Earth and in Heaven, praising their eternal Lord.

The paintings were not only refined in execution, but the painters often showed enormous skill in the selection of motifs and subjects, which were placed in various zones and could correspond not only with the altars but with each other in fascinating ways. The modern strip cartoonist, who can show action only by placing his figures in a row starting at the left and ending on the right, and who has to place the speech in bubbles with "uggh" and "waah", can learn a lot from the talking in these silent pictures.

In 1496 the Romanesque period had been left far behind. We do not know

Fig. 1. The Descent of the Holy Ghost. Bellinge church, the east vault, east cell.

Fig. 2. The Descent of the Holy Ghost, Biblia Pauperum.

how many paintings our painter executed in this church. But we do know, as one of my students demonstrated in a paper some years ago,[1] that he designed some of his paintings in this church according to pictures in the woodcut edition of the Biblia Pauperum. We do not know if he had any more pages from this book than those used in these paintings. But it is certain that he used other models as well. For instance, St George fighting with the dragon (Fig. 5) is not to be found in the *Biblia Pauperum,* and several other features must originate from other sources.

But it is interesting that we can clearly see the tradition as handed down to our painter, and a certain confusion in his mind when he planned the decoration of this church (Fig. 1, Ulla Haastrup). The painter came into the church through the same door as we did, and it was evident to him that the sacred story had to start from the entrance. Therefore you can see some of the stages in the Passion of Christ running in sequence from the entrance in the west to the east. And in the eastern cells of each vault you will find some of the events of Easter and Pentecost in the same chronological order as in the Bible: Jesus praying in Gethsemane (Fig. 9, Ulla Haastrup), the Last Supper (Fig. 2, Ulla Haastrup) and the Descent of the Holy Ghost. You can walk through the entrance and up the nave and feel quite at ease just as in the Sistine Chapel, where Michelangelo executed his creation cycle in the same manner, as he turned all the scenes towards the entrance. The principle was often used in the previous centuries. But it must be noted that what dominates this part of the decoration is the entrance, and not the altar, upon which the Lord himself appears for the congregation.

It is evident that the painter had certain difficulties with the placing of the motifs in the vaults. For the eastern vault he selected from the *Biblia Pauperum* the page depicting the Descent of the Holy ghost (Figs. 1-2). He placed it in the eastern cell because it was the last event in the sacred story, and according to the tradition it had to be placed at the end of the cycle and nearest the altar. As you can see, he omitted the inscriptions on the page, and he was a bit negligent with the prophets, too. But in the execution he only made a few alterations from the page of the *Biblia Pauperum* he had in his hand. It must have been cut from the 40-page edition because in this book the prophet Elias (Fig. 3) is shown to the right of the central scene in the eastern cell and Moses receiving the tables of the law to the left (Fig. 4). On the page from the 50-page edition the order is just the opposite, but the main features are the same.

[1] Jacob Clausen, "Biblen i Bellinge" in *ICO, Den iconographiske Post,* 1974, 1, 3-11.

Fig. 3. The Sacrifice of Elias. Bellinge Church, the east vault, north cell.

Fig. 4. Moses receiving the Tables of the Law. Bellinge church, the east vault, sourth cell.

But then his troubles started, and they are caused by the pages he used. They are two-dimensional, but the room has three dimensions. On the page we have only three pictures, but the vault has four cells. And what he could paint as a fourth motif connected with the Descent of the Holy Ghost had not been explained to him. Instead, he painted the two Spies with the Cluster of Grapes, which tradition never connects with the Descent, but often with the Crucifixion of Christ, which is seen beneath on the northern wall (Fig. 6, Ulla Haastrup). It must be stressed, however, that the *Biblia* does not use this event as a prototype for the execution of Christ. There you will find other themes, the Sacrifice of Isaac, the Adoration of the Brazen Serpent, the Creation of Eve, and Moses striking the Rock. But not the Spies with the Cluster of Grapes.

The model for the Last Supper (Figs. 2 and 11, Ulla Haastrup) is not the corresponding picture in the Biblia. But the scene with the Gathering of Manna in the Desert (Fig. 3, Ulla Haastrup) is depicted in the book to the left of the Supper, but here to the right. The other prototype, King Melchizedek greeting Abraham, is not depicted, perhaps because the painter had no model to use. Perhaps another prototype in the southern cell of the western vault, Isaac carrying the wood to his own Sacrifice (Fig. 5, Ulla Haastrup), originates from the *Biblia Pauperum,* but it is not certain. But as you can see, it has not been placed in any relation to the corresponding theme from the Passion, Christ carrying his cross (Fig. 6), which is placed on the northern wall. In the *Biblia Pauperum* they are placed side by side, according to the tradition (Fig. 10, Ulla Haastrup). As to the paintings of Christ in Gethsemane (Fig. 9, Ulla Haastrup), Christ crowned with Thorns, and the Flagellation of Christ, the painter has not shown any prototypes from the Old Testament. Perhaps he had no models for them.

In retrospect it must be said that the painter was guided by tradition to some degree, and was very dependent on his models. They come from various sources; he did not have many of them, and he did not know how to arrange them according to traditional principles. But as you can see, he was by no means a bad painter, and quite a gifted narrator, who could entertain the congregation, and who gave some dignity to the scenes and figures. But he could not express the sanctity of the church, as it was centred on the presence of the Saviour upon the altar. Other painters in Scandinavia from the same period knew far better. They were better educated and could obtain better theological guidance, which made them capable of painting cycles and series, where both purposes – and very often more than two – were always fulfilled in a great

Fig. 6. The Bearing of the Cross. Note the shooting jester to the right. Bellinge church, the north wall.

homogeneous sequence. It was an admirable art, which still has to be explored in many details, but which will be unforgettable for those who have seen for example Over Dråby on Sjælland, Konga in Skåne, Härnevi in Uppland, and particularly Lojo and Hattula in Southern Finland.

Our painter did not belong to that privileged crowd. Perhaps he was confused by his task, and in his confusion he introduced a book which was in no way intended as a sketch-book for disheartened painters in remote village churches, but was meant to create a pious and devout mind outside the church. Now it came to stress the importance of the same mind inside the church. The book maintained its spell over the mind and was made a substitute for the sanctity and sacredness radiating from the presence of the Lord upon the altar. The accent slowly shifted from the gifts bestowed upon man to what went on inside the human mind. Of course this is only a very small detail in the battle of books which grew with incredible intensity in the following century, promoted by the learned humanists and the reformationists as well. The victory of humanism was the victory of the independent book, even in the Lutheran church. Even here it was soon forgotten that Luther only maintained the Bible as a poor substitute for a congregation who could not hear a Protestant sermon on Sundays. The Bible with its words and stories was treated with a kind of devotion which should only be for God himself. The development could not be stopped. In the diocese of Odense the pure word from the book brought an end to the pictures on the church walls and altars. The wallpaintings in this church were hidden beneath a layer of chalk. There they remained until 1883.

University of Copenhagen

The wall paintings in the parish church of Bellinge (dated 1496) explained by parallels in contemporary European theatre

by ULLA HAASTRUP

The wall paintings in Bellinge church, just outside the city of Odense, were uncovered about 100 years ago. At that time the paintings had been covered by whitewash since about 1590. It is very unusual to have such exact dating of the first whitewashing of a Danish wall painting. Here it is due to the fact that Bishop Jacob Madsen noted in his journal of pastoral visitations in 1589 that he had requested that the paintings should be whitewashed and in 1596 that it had been done.[1] As a rule the wall paintings were not whitewashed directly after the Danish Reformation in 1536, this step not being taken until the introduction of Pietism in the eighteenth century. Perhaps the very didactic structure of the picture sequence appeared just as Catholic and dangerous in the bishop's eyes as the religious theatre must have appeared to the Church of England after the Reformation, as both the religious plays and the wall paintings had the same clear purpose of religious teaching.[2]

The wall-paintings in Bellinge today appear in a somewhat deteriorated condition with several repaintings from the last century, which do seem, however to reproduce the original pictures. The paintings must have been quite well preserved when found, having only been exposed to view for a hundred years.[3]

This goes for the three vaults of the nave, the northern wall of the nave, and for the ornamentation in the vault of the chancel. The paintings in the chancel were only fragmentary, and were whitewashed again without any water colours being made of the only preserved motif, the Transfiguration. The restorer found a painting of Christ with Moses and Elijah but he did not record

[1] Hans Jørgen Frederiksen, "Kalkmalerierne og billedproblemet i den danske Kirke 1536-ca. 1600", *Ico* 3, Stockholm 1979, p. 14-24.

[2] Gardiner, H. C., S. J., *Mysteries' End. An Investigation of the Last Days of the Medieval Religious Stage*. 2nd ed. Hamden, Conn., 1967.

[3] Descriptions from the uncovering of the wall-paintings made by Jacob Kornerup 1883 and water colours also by him as well as all later material concerning Bellinge church are in Dept. Two of the National Museum, Copenhagen.

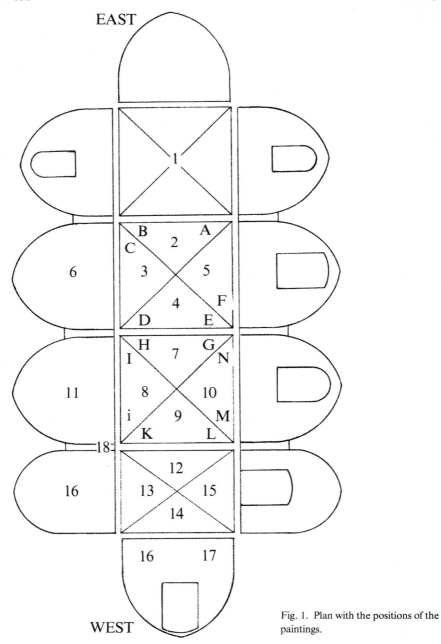

EAST

WEST

Fig. 1. Plan with the positions of the paintings.

Bellinge church

1. The Transfiguration (unknown position in the vault)
2. The Descent of the Holy Ghost
3. The Offering of Elijah
4. The Scout of Joshua
5. Moses receiving the Tables of the law
6. The Croucifixion
7 The Last Supper
8. The Gathering of Manna
9. The Ascension
10. Christ before Pilate
11. The Bearing of the Cross
12. The Agony in the Garden
13. The Flagellation
14. Christ Crowned with Thorns
15. Isaac and Abraham on their Way to the Offering
16. Saint George and the Dragon, The King and Queen in the Castle
17. Saint Christopher (nearly invisible)
18. Inscription with date and names of the painters

A. Nameless figure (prophet?)
B. "Davit"
C. Nameless figure (prophet?)
D. Nameless figure (prophet?)
E. Nameless figure (prophet?)
F. Jester
G. Nameless figure (prophet?)
H. Nameless figure (prophet?)
I. "Davit"
J. "Zorobabel" (Serubabel)
K. Nameless figure (prophet?)
L. Nameless figure (prophet?)
M. Nameless figure (prophet?)
N. Nameless figure (prophet?)

---

in which vault cell it was painted. The paintings on the southern wall of the nave were destroyed when the windows were enlarged.

As is clear from the plan with the positioning of the motifs (fig. 1) any biblical chronology seems to have been lost. In the chancel there must have been scenes from the life of Christ and the three vaults in the nave have motifs from the passion of Christ.

St George's fight with the dragon (fig. 5, Banning) is now the only depiction in Bellinge of a Christian martyr. The huge picture on the northern and western walls of the nave below the tower has been placed in a way very similar to other late Gothic pictures of St George. Rather extraordinary is that there apparently are two princesses (a big one and a small one) both with a lamb on a leash. The explanation apparently is that the painters originally painted the small one and then either changed their minds or were ordered to paint a bigger one. The brown ochre of the bigger one's dress must have covered the little princess completely. But when the painting was uncovered, both drawings must have come forward equally clearly, and consequently the restorer left them both on view. At the western wall of the nave near the entrance there are now only small fragments of a picture of Saint Christopher left.

On the pier next to St George and the dragon there is a long and very interesting inscription telling us that the painters Ebbe Olsen and Simon Petersen painted these pictures in 1496.[4] Unfortunately this kind of signed and dated works are very unusual in Danish late Gothic wall-paintings. It is often guessed that two or more painters did the paintings, but usually there is no evidence, as there are practically no written sources describing wallpainters or their workshops in Denmark.[5]

In Bellinge we have the opportunity to detect the painters' working methods, since they must have used printed models for most of the scenes. Jacob Clausen has pointed out in *Den iconographiske Post* that several of the scenes are modelled on woodcuts from the *Biblia Pauperum*,[6] (cf. Knud Banning p. 128). This practice was probably very common in Northern Europe in the late middle ages, where the desire for originality and naturalism was almost unknown.[7]

The problem for the two painters was probably that they had some good models which were conceptually connected in groups of three. Anyone can imagine the difficulty of using these in quartered vaults. It appears from the plan that the Pentecost, Elijah's sacrifice, and Moses receiving the tables of

[4] "Anno d(omi)ni millesimo qvadringentesimo nonagesimo sex(t)o h(ae)c pictura c(om)pleta fvit per man(us) ebonis olai et simonis petri".

[5] See *Søren Kaspersen, p. 157 ff.*

[6] Jacob Clausen, "Biblen i Bellinge. Et eksempel på Biblia Pauperums anvendelse i dansk kalkmaleri", *Ico* 1, København 1974. He describes specifically the motives of The Last Supper, Moses receiving the Tables of the Law, and the Offering of Elijah, but mentions too that the Fall of Manna, Abraham and Isaac on their way to the Sacrifice, The Ascension and the Bearing of the Cross have models in the printed pictures in the *Biblia Pauperum.*

Fig. 2. The Last Supper. Bellinge church.

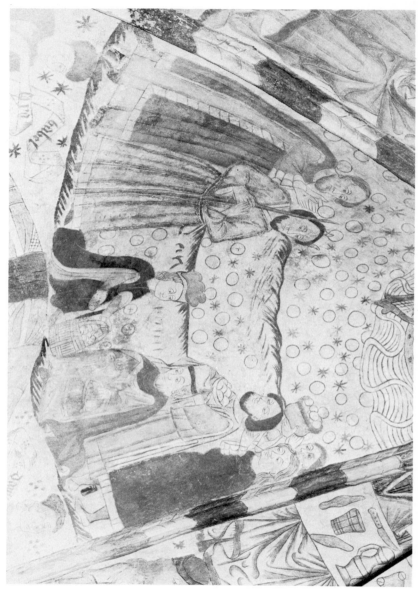

Fig. 3. The Gathering of the Manna. Bellinge church.

the Law belong together in the first vault counting from the east. In the second vault, east cell, is the institution of the Holy Communion (fig. 2), connected with the Spies with the Cluster of Grapes in the west cell in the first vault, and the Gathering of Manna (fig. 3), north cell of the second vault. The Presentation before Pilate, south cell, and the Ascension (fig. 4) west cell, same vault, like the three motives in the third vault, The Prayer in the Garden of Gethsemane, east cell, the Scourging, north cell and the Crowning with Thorns west cell have no typology from the Old Testament. In the south cell third vault, however, there is one motif, Abraham and Isaac on their way to the Sacrifice (fig. 5) which is typologically connected to the Bearing of the Cross (fig. 6, Banning), on the north wall, second vault. In the first part of the north wall is the Crucifixion (fig. 6), but no connected typological motifs have been preserved.

Besides the biblical motifs there are in the pendentives of the cells some prophet figures and in the south cell of the first vault a fool with a tambourine (fig. 7).

This fool together with the fool in the scene of the Bearing of the Cross (fig. 6, Banning) has long been famous in Danish theatrical history,[8] being presented as examples of the appearance of the Danish medieval fool. But considering the printed German or Dutch models after which all the paintings were executed, a certain caution must be exercised when drawing parallels to Danish fools. On the other hand it is clear that the two painters must have recognised them by their requisites and behaviour and known that the congregation would do so just as if they had been ordinary Danish fools. We have now entered a very complicated field in which the foreign models of many of the Danish wallpaintings preclude us from using the paintings as purely Danish source material. To a great extent this applies to the biblical motifs as well, especially when looking at these in a theatrical connection, as is my intention in this small essay.

The fool in the pendentive (fig. 7) has been painted slightly bent as if sitting on the rib, beating a tambourine. The head is painted in profile and he is wearing a typical fool's cap with ass's ears and stockings, one red, the other green.

In the scene of the Bearing of the Cross the fool has been painted in front of the procession and after him follows the soldier who is leading Christ by a

---

[7] See Ulla Haastrup, "Kalkmaleri i Viskinge og kunst i Westfalen", *Nationalmuseets Arbejdsmark* 1967 and same, "En europæisk madonnatype og to kalkmalerier i Brunnby", *En bog om Kunst til Else Kai Sass*, København 1978.

[8] Torben Krogh, *Ældre dansk Teater*, København 1940, p. 19 ff.

Fig. 4. The Ascension. Bellinge church.

Fig. 5. Abraham and Isaac on their way to the Sacrifice. Bellinge church.

Fig. 6. The Crucifixion. Bellinge church.

Fig. 8. The fool Nis Gieck.
Wall painting in Dråby church, Jutland.

Fig. 7. A fool with a tambourine.
Bellinge church.

rope, "The Ductor" as he is called in the German passion plays. Again the fool is wearing a fool's cap with ears and scallops at the edge. He is blowing a horn and holding a gun firing three bullets. This fool has been painted in profile too. The imagined loud noise from the gun and the horn is designed to call attention. Both in connection with the passion plays and the contemporary trials such heralds were used to announce the approach either of Christ bearing the cross or an actual criminal on his way to the place of execution. The two events, the ecclesiastical theatre and the public execution were closely knit.[9] Thus the theatrical processions in the city of York are known to have ended at the normal place of execution where the crucifixion would be represented.

[9] The Barbara Altar in St Mary's Church, Gdansk. Barbara is led naked through the streets to the place of execution. In front of her is a fool with a bagpipe. Willi Drost, *Die Marienkirche in Danzig und ihre Kunstschätze,* Stuttgart 1963, fig. 129.

The pure profile of the two fools expresses the wickedness of the persons, as for example the executioner. There were strict rules in the Middle Ages as to how different people should be painted, for example the angle of the head. The ordinary position was three-quarter face, only divine persons in majestic positions like Christ in Judgement on the rainbow were depicted in full face.[10] Evil persons, like executioners and devils were painted in profile, and thus the fools as well. The fool in the Bearing of the Cross is easy to understand, but the lonely fool in the pendentive beneath Moses receiving the law, is somewhat harder to account for. Perhaps he should be related to the Jews or possibly the contemporary concept of the unworthy actor. The wall-painting – perhaps a portrait of the fool Nis Gieck (fig. 8) – in Dråby church on Mols is painted in profile too.[11] This division of persons into bad, ordinary, good, or divine according to the position of their heads made it much easier for the layman to conceive the meaning of the picture.

Similarly the costumes of the persons corresponded to contemporary costumes and armour. Prophets wear learned costumes while Elijah is dressed as a monk. Only holy persons are dressed in "archaic" clothes, Christ and the apostles are barefooted. These costumes and the haloes of the holy persons made them very distinctive.

Finally the requisites made the action of the different scenes clear, for example the Prayer in the Garden of Gethsemane, where Christ is praying in the garden, symbolized by a wattle and a rock ("nature"). His prayer "Let this cup pass from me" is represented in the iconographic tradition and the theatrical tradition by a cup placed before Christ with a small cross on it symbolizing his imminent Passion. These symbolic requisites clearly show the spectator of both the paintings and the theatre the meaning of the words and the action.

Here we are concerned with the artistic effects in the wallpaintings and their connection with their models and the medieval ecclesiastical plays. Since Émil Mâle in the beginning of this century described the influence of the medieval theatre on contemporary art, people have been discussing which genre was the first.[12] When Rosemary Woolf in her important book on British miracle plays

---

[10] Ulla Haastrup,"Kristus en face = Deus Majestatis", *Kristusfremstillinger*, Foredrag holdt ved det 5. nordiske symposium for ikonografiske studier på Fuglsang 29. aug.-3. sept. 1976. Red. Ulla Haastrup. København 1980.

[11] Ulla Haastrup, *Påskespil og Kirkekunst.* Udstillingskatalog, Nationalmuseet 1974.

[12] Émile Mâle, *L'Art Religieux de la fin du moyen âge en France. Étude sur l'iconographie du moyen âge et sur ses sources d'inspiration,* Paris 1905. Else Kai Sass, "Pilate and the Title for Christ's Cross in Medieval Representations of Golgotha", *Hafnia,* Copenhagen Papers in the History of Art, 1972, Copenhagen 1974.

discusses the development of the characteristic cycles of plays, she assumes that the cycles, so to say, are merely catching up on the already existing tradition for long picture programmes based on certain selected biblical themes.[13]

Generally these discussions of who was the earlier and who influenced who appear to me to be completely misleading. It is generally important to realize that both plays and wallpaintings as well as sculptures and book-illustrations had important didactic tasks to perform for the church. The presentation of the themes often has to be identical because of the fact that the actors on the cart, on the square, or in the church had to use pictures and symbols known to their audience.[14] On the other hand the strict iconographic tradition must have bound the majority of the artists. Only a few – like the von Eyck-brothers or Rogier van der Weyden – created new iconogaphic types often by combining old traditions.

In a few cases it is even possible to show direct borrowings from one genre to another, sometimes creating new traditions. It is, however, often difficult to prove, because of the fragmentary character of our material both in texts and pictures, thus a "new type" may not exist in the Scandinavian material but be quite common in French sources.

In working with the iconography of Danish wall-paintings I have often found that English, German, or French theatrical texts to at great extent can explain the content and meaning of the pictures in the churches. They provide us with the missing context, as is often the case with contemporary sermons, as Anne Riising has showed here at Bellinge.[15]

The specific motifs of the church paintings can by very interesting and provide information on certain aspects of society, such as tools, clothing, style, figure composition, and the imitation of nature and so on. Of course the picture analyses of the specific motifs is important but the juxtaposition of different scenes may also be of great importance. It is necessary to try to understand what the pictures might have meant to the contemporary onlooker, but it may of course be as hard to understand as the "Haiko poems" are to us West-Europeans. The superficial meaning seems clear to us but all the import-

---

[13] Rosemary Woolf, *The English Mystery Plays,* Berkeley and Los Angeles 1972, pp. 54-76.

[14] Ulla Haastrup, "Kalkmalerier og senmiddelalderens spil – belyst ved en 1500-tals udmaling af Sulsted kirke i Jylland", *Fra Sankt Olav til Martin Luther,* Foredrag fremlagt ved det tredje nordiske symposium for ikonografiske studier, Bårdshaug, den 21.-24. aug. 1972, Oslo 1975.

[15] Anne Riising, "Om Bellinge kirkes kalkmalerier. Ord og billeder i middelalderlig forkyndelse". *Fyns stiftsbog* 1972, Odense 1972 pp. 7-27. Same, *Danmarks middelalderlige Prædiken,* Disputats, Odense 1969.

ant associations to earlier poetry, the symbolic value of the single words and the impression of the original calligraphy are lost to us.

A wallpainting programme as in Bellinge presumably had several layers of possible perception in those days. The illiterate peasant with little knowledge of the theological use of typology probably did not "read" the pictures the same way the theologian from the city of Odense did. Among other things the texts must have had a very different impact on the uneducated and the learned spectators.

Both to the wallpainter and the makers of the models the primary need must have been to make the meaning of the pictures clear, cf. the Prayer in the Garden of Gethsemane, (p. 146). Exactly the same need was felt by the actor in the ecclesiastical plays of the late middle ages but here the mother tongue and the movements of the actors helped the spectator to understand the meaning of the plays.

Comparing the available Danish written evidence with the European material there has probably not been any Danish passion plays, but again the Danish evidence is sparse.

On the other hand there is actual "archeological proof" of the existence of liturgical plays: several Easter sepulchres and a single Danish Ascension figure, used in the celebration of the Ascension, exist.[16] In view of the conditions in other European countries it seems very unlikely that Denmark as the sole country had no plays, though the actual material, the texts, with only a few exceptions is lacking.

So when drawing parallels to theatrical texts in my interpretation of the wallpaintings, these must not be regarded as proving the existence of ecclesiastical plays in Denmark. The impact of the models is too strong to do that, and generally the wall-painters of the late Gothic period did not reproduce "reality", and thus not the reality of the plays. The thesis that "a wall-painting reproduces persons, things, and actions from other pictures" is almost the whole truth.

The motif of Abraham and Isaac (fig. 5) on their way to the Offering of Isaac is closely related to the picture in the woodcut of *Biblia Pauperum* (fig. 10). There are only two other wall-paintings left in Denmark with this motif: in Fanefjord church on Møn painted by the Elmelunde workshop between 1500-1520 and in Gjøl church north of the Limfjord in Jutland painted around 1530.[17] In both cases the story is continued to the happy ending. In Bellinge the

---

[16] Ulla Haastrup, "Kristi himmelfartsspil i Visby", *Fornvännen* Årg. 68, pp. 37-48, Stockholm 1973. Also note 11.

[17] Kalkmaleriregistranten, Nationalmuseet, København.

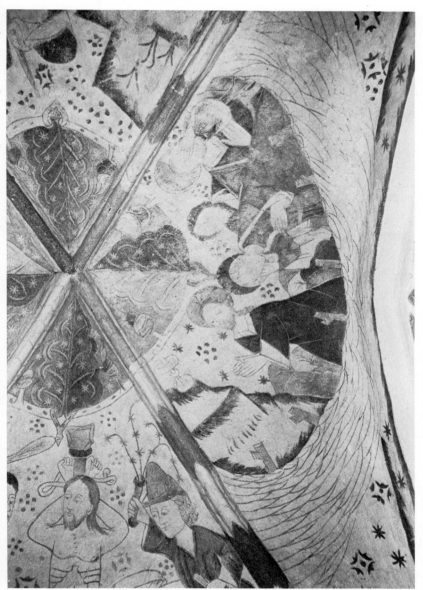

Fig. 9. The Prayer in the Garden of Gethsemane. Bellinge church.

Fig. 10. *Biblia Pauperum.* The bearing of the Cross and to the left Abrahan and Isaac on their way to the Sacrifice.

stress is clearly put on the parallel between the Old Testament with the good son carrying the wood for his own sacrifice, and the New Testament with Christ carrying his wooden cross. In early pictures the wood of Isaac was even made into a cross to emphasize the typology.[18]

Abraham and Isaac in Bellinge look very much like the woodcut in *Biblia Pauperum* and differ only in a few details, which are nevertheless important. Abraham is not carrying the big theatrical scimitar as in the woodcut and the long candle has been made into a walking-stick by the restorer, forgetting that medieval sticks did not look like that, but had a straight perpendicular handle.[19]

The requisites are very important in this scene. A British play from York vividly describes how the heavy wood is transported on an ass but at the foot of the mountain the heavy burden is laid upon the shoulders of the poor Isaac by the otherwise loving farther. He himself is carrying the "murder weapon" and the fire for the sacrificial pyre.[20] The painters in Bellinge, in accordance with the printed model, have given Abraham a huge altar candle as his "fire". An unmistakable requisite in plays and in wall-paintings, but extremely unrealistic, since the light would have gone out before Abraham got halfway up the mountain. On the other hand the burning candle probably is a quite suitable requisite. The big scimitar has in Bellinge become a much more significant requisite, namely a sharp-pointed curved butchers knife hanging in Abraham's belt. So it is stressed that Abraham is going to slaughter his own son as a sacrificial animal.[21] The sympathy of the congregation must have been strong for the poor father and his good son, even without the touching conversation that for instance appears in the Brome play.[22]

[18] Isaac with two crossed pieces of wood on his shoulder. Abraham with his sword drawn on the shoulder and a torch in his hand. Misericord in Worcester Cathedral. M. D. Anderson, *History and Imagery in British Churches*. London 1971, fig. 9.

[19] In the wallpaintings in Fanefjord Abraham holds both a candle and a stick with a straight perpendicular handle. The big sword is held under his right arm.

[20] "Abraham: ... Children, bide ye here still./ No further shall ye go./ For yonder I see the hill/ That we shall wend unto.
Isaak: Keep well our ass and all our gear./ To time we come again to you.
Abraham: My son, this wood behoves thee bear./ Till thou come high upon yon hill. "J. S. Purvis, *The York Cycle of Mystery Plays*. London 1978, paperback ed. p. 61f.

[21] Parenthetically it can be mentioned that the Sacrifice of Isaac in the play in Newcastle upon Tyne according to the records was performed by the butchers of the town. Hardin Craig, *English Religious Drama of the Middle Ages*. Oxford 1955, p. 304.

[22] For the text of the Brome play see Peter Happé ed., *English Mystery Plays*, Penguin, Harmondsworth 1975, pp. 152-170.

Fig. 11. *Biblia Pauperum*. The Last Supper and to the right The Gathering of the Manna.

As mentioned above there are two typologies on the Communion, The Spies with the Cluster of Grapes and the Gathering of Manna. In Bellinge both scenes have models in *Biblia Pauperum* (fig. 11), but concerning the manna (fig. 3) the painters have made the meaning of the scene more clear to the congregation. The heavenly manna saving the Jews from starvation in the desert is depicted as small circular objects, exactly like the printed model. But in Bellinge there are small crosses visible on some of them, giving them a clear resemblance to the Host.

The Communion-scene in Bellinge (fig. 2) does not completely follow the *Biblia Pauperum* print (fig. 11). Most important is that the table in the print is round with the apostles spread around it, whereas the table in the wall-painting is a long one and the apostles, partly modelled after the print, are placed on both sides of Christ, sitting with the sleeping John on his lap. A quite common iconographic explanation of the ancient table manners: lying at the table. Opposite Christ is Judas identified by his usual requisite, the purse attached to his belt, and an evil profile with his mouth open. On the table in front of Christ lie the paschal lamb and bread, with a small heap of circular objects, and Christ is offering Judas one of these objects, which is marked with a cross. It is of course a host, exactly like the hosts in the Gathering of the Manna.

As a result the meaning of the picture changes fundamentally. From being a depiction of the Institution of the Communion suddenly it becomes an indication of the sinfulness of Judas, too. From the text of the English Communion play form the *Ludus Conventriae,* we can gather the meaning of the scene.[23]
Whan eure Lord gyvyth his body to his Dyscypulys he xal sey to eche of hem, except to Judas.
Jesus: This is my body, flesch and blode,/ That for the xal dey up-on rode.
And whan Judas comyth last, oure Lord xal sey to hym.
Jesus: Judas, art thou avysyd what thou xalt take?
Judas: Lord, thi body I wyl not for-sake.
And sythyn oure Lord wal sey on-to Judas.
Jesus: Myn body to the I wole not deye,/ Sythyn thou wylt presume ther-upon;/ Yt xal be thi dampnacyon verylye,/ I geve the warnyng now be-forn.
And aftyr that Judas hath reseyvyd he xal syt ther he was, Chryst seyng.
On of you hath be-trayd me,/ That at my borde me hate ete:/ Bettyr it hadde hym for to a be/ Bothe un-born and un-begete.

In this text the emphasis is placed upon Judas making himself guilty of an unforgivable sin by accepting the Communion like the other apostles, without

---

[23] The Last Supper Play in the *Ludus Conventriae* see op. cit. Happé, p. 432-455.

having confessed his sins though being carefully questioned by Christ. In *Ludus Conventriae* and in Bellinge there is a strong warning to the congregation not to receive Communion before having confessed their sins, since they will otherwise invoke eternal damnation like Judas[24]. The motif in Bellinge placed in the important eastern square of the vault thus shows not only the historical event of the institution of the Communion but has a further message to the congregation. In the theatre this could be told orally, here in Bellinge the painters have changed their model and brought in another tradition and have in this way put additional meaning into the motifs.[25]

The Ascension (fig. 4) is quite faithful to the printed models of *Biblia Pauperum* (fig. 12) and to the contemporary iconographic tradition. The apostles are grouped on both sides of a little hill, with the footprints of Christ on it. Christ has almost ascended to heaven only the lowest part of his coat and his naked feet are still visible under the edging (symbol of heaven). Behind both the pictorial and the theatrical tradition – in the Ascension of the Chester play where the stage direction says: "..stabit Jhesus in medio quasi supra nubes" – is the knowledge of the liturgical Ascension plays[26]. Here a fullscale sculpture of Christ in painted wood was lifted up through a hole in the vault, while the clergy were singing the lines of the apostles and of Mary, and a man hidden under "the mountain with the footprints" was singing the lines of Christ. Such traditions in liturgical plays can be traced back as far as the second half of the thirteenth century here in Scandinavia. We know that these plays must have been performed in Denmark too, because one of these sculptures has been

---

[24] A similar line of thought can be seen in the fragment "Quire P.". Stanley J. Kahrl, *Traditions of Medieval English Drama,* London 1974, p. 66f.

[25] A very close iconographical parallel to the Communion scene in Bellinge with the twelve hosts on the table and Christ offering Judas one is found in the wallpaintings in Gislinge, Zealand, a contemporary decoration. Already in 1437 in the wallpaintings in Tensta, Sweden, Christ offers Judas a host, but no other hosts are found on the table. Actually the most logical depiction, following the text of the plays, where all the apostles receive their hosts first. And Judas eats his as the last one. Also outside Scandinavia pictures of the Last Supper appear where the Communion character of the meal is explicitly indicated by adding hosts to the ordinary pascal meal. A good example of this is the predella painted by Hans Murer d. Ä. (1486/87) for the Augustinerchorherrenstift Kreuzlingen, Thurgau. Christ is holding a host in his raised right hand, in front of him stands a chalice and a small heap of hosts on the table. Judas, in profile, is kneeling at the table but is not receiving the host from Christ, who has the appearance of a priest celebrating Mass and is seen full face. Margrit Früh, "Die Abendmahlstafel in Frauenfelde in Werk von Hans Murer d. Ä.", *Zeitschrift für Schweizerich Archäologie und Kunstgeschichte.* Band 36, Heft 4, Zürich 1979, pp. 239-247.

[26] The Ascension play from Chester. op. cit. Happé pp. 607-615, especially p. 611.

Fig. 12. *Biblia Pauperum*. The Ascension.

preserved in Kirke-Helsinge church on Zealand (now in the Danish National Museum).[27]

Several other motifs in Bellinge could be analysed in a similar way, but I hope that this brief treatment of some of the pictures has been sufficient to indicate my working methods.

A *Biblia Pauperum* consists partly of pictures, and partly of long texts, some of which are held by prophets. The prophets in Bellinge hold these inscription scrolls as well, but they contain nothing but the names of the figures. Not even in the actual biblical scenes are the pictures and the texts combined as in the prints. Long inscription scrolls appear, but the texts are often quite unusual in the contexts they are placed in, for example the Bearing of the Cross: "misere nobis dom(ine) Jh (esu Christe)" a prayer that may appear strange in the context. Likewise the text in the Crucifixion is very unusual.

Below the big paintings on the walls there is a long inscription which unfortunately has not yet been deciphered. Perhaps some of the missing *Biblia Pauperum* texts might be found here. But generally the wall-paintings in Bellinge have lost the textual explanation of the motifs, compared to the almost contemporary paintings in Hjembæk church, Zealand,[28] which are modelled on *Biblia Pauperum* too, both figures and texts. Thus a prophet in Hjembæk is seated on a calyx connected with the Crucifixion scene. He is holding an inscription scroll, the text of which tells the history of Abraham and Isaac. The actual motif has not been depicted.

The paintings in Bellinge therefore need a special interpretation that can be achieved by using late medieval ecclesiastical plays from other countries. Only in this way a full understanding of the specific painted motifs and their internal connection can be achieved.

University of Copenhagen

---

[27] Note 16 and 11 with a figure of the Ascension Christ from Kirke-Helsinge.

[28] Niels Saxtorph, *Jeg ser på kalkmalerier*, 3. udg. København 1979, p. 116f.

The wall paintings at Bellinge and their group

by Søren Kaspersen

The wall paintings in Bellinge Church[1] are dated and signed in an inscription on the north engaged pier between the nave and the tower bay which reads: Anno, d(omi)ni, millesimo quadringentesimo nonagesimo, sex(to), h(æc) pictura (com)pleta fuit, per man(us) ebonis olai et simonis petri. The names Ebbe Olsen and Simon Petersen are not known from other churches, and it is certainly no longer possible to distinguish between the two artists' work at Bellinge. On the other hand the paintings are clearly connected with more other decorations, primarily the murals in the south chapel in Kirke-Stillinge Church in south-west Zealand[2] and a fragment, now again covered, on the arch of the nave arcade leading into the south chapel of Finderup Church[3] about ten kilometres north-east of Kirke-Stillinge. The fragment was most likely part of a larger decoration and showed a female saint with a sword and a book, probably St Catherine. Her dress was of somewhat less confident execution than is in evidence at Kirke-Stillinge.

Wall paintings related to this group are, however, also found outside the present borders of the country. An inscription in Linderöd Church in the east of Scania records that the extensive decoration, which is preserved in the vaulting of the chancel and nave – and no doubt also covered the walls – was painted in 1498 by Andreas Johannis, or Anders Johansson.[4] The same artist also worked in Färlöv Church about 20 kilometres north-east of Linderöd, but here the surviving section of the originally extensive paintings, namely those in

---

[1] Uncovered in 1883 and restored by J. Kornerup in 1884. The report material for this and other Danish wall paintings is in the topographical archive in Department Two of the National Museum.

[2] Uncovered in 1864 and restored in 1868 by J. Kornerup. See *Danmarks Kirker*, V:2, Sorø Amt (Copenhagen 1938) 726-27.

[3] Revealed when the south chapel arch was reopened in 1925.

[4] Finally uncovered and restored by O. Owald 1950-51. See *A Catalogue of Wall-Paintings in the Churches of Medieval Denmark, 1100-1600, Scania Halland Blekinge*, ed. K. Banning I-III (Copenhagen 1976), vol. II, 258-62 – hereafter referred to as Cat. SHB.

the chancel vault, have been heavily restored.[5] The stylistic connection between these two examples was pointed out as early as 1952 by Monica Rydbeck.[6] But at the same time many features point to a connection between Andreas Johannis' paintings and the Bellinge group. Moreover a further link between the two groups is found in the wall paintings in the old choir in Östra Strö Church in central Scania.[7] Amongst Scanian murals their closest parallels are at Linderöd and Färlöv, but the similarities with Bellinge and Kirke-Stillinge are at least as striking.

A detailed account of the Scanian wall paintings and their connection with the Bellinge group is in the course of preparation.[8] The present treatment will therefore be confined to an indication of the most important common features of the various decorations. The faces in all of them have a marked graphic character. The sharp outline often causes the jaw to protrude noticeably. The eyes are usually small with heavy lids. The cleft under the nose is indicated by two strokes. The hair is sometimes painted but more often represented by parallel strokes. The most substantial difference between the faces of the Bellinge group and those of Andreas Johannis is probably that the latter does not draw eyebrows. In Östra Strö the faces have eyebrows, and the best of them are very similar to those at Bellinge. The representation of the hair in the Linderöd figures is more meticulous than at Kirke-Stillinge, while at Bellinge it seems to have been made somewhat looser in restoration. At Östra Strö it is only fragmentarily preserved and at Färlöv it has been completely distorted by repainting.

Characteristic of the draperies at Bellinge are masses of rounded folds giving a loose, complex and sometimes fluid effect. The materials change tone from dark shading in their basic colour to areas approximating to highlights. The same form of shading is seen at Kirke-Stillinge, though the folds are more orderly, no doubt owing to more sensitive restoration. Andreas Johannis' draperies seem generally simpler, and he does not use highlights. That they are nevertheless related to those of the Bellinge group is seen from a comparison of St Olav at Linderöd (Fig. 2) with the Angel of the Annunciation at Kirke-Stillinge (Fig. 1), and again with St Thomas at Östra Strö (Fig. 3).

[5] Uncovered in 1882 and restored in 1905 by A. Persson Waldur. See Cat. SHB, II, 138-40.

[6] M. Rydbeck, Anders Johansson, en svensk konstnär från unionstidens Skåne, *Konsthistorisk Tidskrift* XXI, 1952, 13-25 (summary in German).

[7] Uncovered and restored in 1930 by H. Erlandsson. See Cat. SHB, III, 282-83.

[8] In a fourth volume of Cat. SHB with an art-historical survey by the present writer with the collaboration of Ulla Haastrup.

Fig. 1. The Annunciation. Vault of St Anne's Chapel(?), north cell. Kirke-Stillinge Church.

Fig. 2. St Olav. Chancel
vault, north cell west.
Linderöd Church.

Fig. 3. St Thomas and donor. The old chancel vault, south cell. Östra Strö Church.

At Kirke-Stillinge the figures appear on a narrow strip of solidly painted ground with small parasol-like trees. At Bellinge on the other hand the surface of the ground is drawn up in successive layers with distinct ridges and small patches of grass. Linderöd and Färlöv show a similar representation of landscape, though in a more restrained version. Even closer to Bellinge is the representation of the soil at Östra Strö, where we see the same strong colouring of the ridges and the angular build-up of the ground (Fig. 3), which is also familiar from several scenes at Bellinge. Finally it must be mentioned that Bellinge also shows examples of another type of natural ground, consisting of mounds of various colours, a characteristic also found in the large Everlöv-Brarup-Elmelunde group of contemporary date[9].

The scattered ornaments on the background space at Bellinge consist of dot rosettes, quadratic corollas and stars, but at Kirke-Stillinge there are only dot rosettes – as in Finderup? At Linderöd the background ornamentation is more loosely drawn and abundantly varied, thus appearing denser. Again we find stars, dot rosettes and quadratic corollas, and a large number of variations on these as well as heads of flowers. At Färlöv the background ornamentation is

[9] The group is treated in more detail in the volume mentioned in the previous note.

again more fixed in character; in the surviving paintings it consists almost exclusively of quadratic corollas, though it originally included dot rosettes, pomegranate figures and a few stars. At Östra Strö dot rosettes are apparently used alone on the vaulting surfaces, but quadratic corollas alternate with these on the underside of a couple of arches.

On the small cells of the vaulting in the latter church there was not room for ornament in the top area. At Linderöd the tops of the cells are filled out with heart-shaped ornaments consisting of two large stylized folded acanthus leaves placed back to back and springing from thick stems. Around the neck of these a cluster of foliage may be suspended by a chain of stems. Where space allows the large leaves are flanked by two smaller trefoils and the whole background of the ornament may be cross-hatched. A variation of this upper ornament is found at Bellinge and Kirke-Stillinge, here in the form of a large acanthus leaf flanked by two pointed spirals against a star-studded background, which at Bellinge is painted in colours. Färlöv on the other hand occupies a special position with its fanciful flowers, some of which spring upwards from a circular stem in the top of the vault, while others form a luxuriant pendant.

To these comparisons may be added other linking characteristics such as the long phylacteries with many folds which appear in the four large decorations. We are thus confronted with a group of paintings which are obviously connected, even though they also exhibit a number of differences and according to the inscriptions were not produced under the direction of a single artist. It is difficult to say what kind of organization is represented by the group as the paintings themselves are our only source of information. It is true that we know many other late medieval groups of wall paintings but conditions vary somewhat from group to group. The size of the workshops and the organization of the work seem to be variable, as well as the individual workshops may be subject to different processes of development and splintering off. Against this background it is very difficult to isolate a workshop at all. Have we in the Linderöd-Bellinge group a large workshop with at least three masters with one or more anonymous assistants, two workshops with a common origin or some third solution?

The paintings at Linderöd and Färlöv have distinguishing features compared with those in Bellinge, Kirke-Stillinge and Finderup, but there are also differences between Bellinge and Kirke-Stillinge, and when do these differences indicate a new workshop? The decoration of Östra Strö shows how complicated the matter can be. It seems most likely that it was painted by people who had connections with the Bellinge workshop, as is shown particularly by

Fig. 4. Day of Judgement.
Apse vault. Östra Strö
Church.

the drawing of the faces and the ground and also by the high narrow gate to
the heavenly Jerusalem of the Day of Judgement scene outermost to the north
of the apse vault adjacent to the tribune arch (Fig. 4) in the same way as the
tower-like buildings at Kirke-Stillinge reach up along the ribs of the vault (Fig.
1). But at the same time the artist is conversant with Scanian traditions, as St
Peter, who admits the saved to the celestial city, wears a tiara, a trait which is
taken from the so-called Vittskövle group.[10] Andreas Johannis also has connections with this group of paintings or more broadly to the Bridgettine artistic
tradition they represent.[11] This is particularly clear in the Creation series at
Linderöd where some of the scenes follow quite closely the iconography we
know from the Vittskövle workshop's Genesis cycles. In view of these complicated relations within the Bellinge-Linderöd group it is probably most reason-
able to guess at offshoots from a workshop or to talk about a group of work-

    [10] See Cat. SHB, I, 153-56, type 12.
    [11] See for example B. G. Söderberg, *De gotländska passionsmålningarna och deras stilfränder. Stu-
dier i birgittinskt muralmåleri* (Stockholm 1942) 148ff. and S. Kaspersen, "Munkelivpsalterens
figurinitialer. Deres forhold til teksten og det birgittinske vægmaleri", *Genesis Profita. Nordiska
Studier i gammeltestamentlig ikonografi*. Acta 33, Stockholm 1980, 186-220, ill.

shops which might be extended to form a school including other groups of paintings, for example the decorations in the monastery of the Holy Spirit at Aalborg and in the churches at Lime, Skelum, Gunderup, Sebber, Tornby and perhaps also Vadum.[12]

The use of certain motifs based on the same models is often a strong indication of the establishment of a workshop. But the Linderöd-Bellinge group is difficult to account for also in this respect, since it is not characterized by repeated series of subjects as for example the Vittskövle group and several other late medieval groups. In fact none of the decorations resemble one another. At Linderöd we find saints in the chancel vault and in the chancel arch while the vaults of the nave is filled by a Genesis series together with some scenes from the life of Christ, martyrdoms, saints and prophets. In Färlöv Church there was originally a Day of Judgement scene in the vault of the apse connected with the 15 signs before the Last Judgement in the vaulting of the chancel and nave, and various scenes including some from the life of Christ on the walls of the nave. At Östra Strö there is also a Day of Judgement in the apse, but here it is supplemented by apostles and St Francis as interceders in the chancel vault. At Kirke-Stillinge we find scenes from the childhood of Mary and Jesus, with Anne, Mary and the Infant Jesus as the protagonists. The paintings most likely embellish the chapel of St Anne, which was endowed at the church c. 1400 by Jens Pedersen of Kelstrup and his wife Kristine.[13]

The paintings inspired by the *Biblia Pauperum* in Bellinge Church are thus unique in the group. It must be added, however, that under the signs before the Last Judgement in the chancel vault at Färlöv there are eight prophets predicting the Day of Judgement with prophecies taken from the *Biblia Pauperum*. And in the pendentives of the first vault of the nave at Linderöd we also find prophets with phylacteries, but they have become too faint to identify. While the programme of the other churches is comparatively easy to determine, the introduction of the typologically charged motifs at Bellinge seems somewhat confusing. However, there is a striking concentration of motifs which speak of the foundation and expansion of the church (the Ascension and Pentecost with types) and of its Sacraments (the Last Supper, the Gathering of Manna and the two Spies with the Cluster of Grapes) in the two vaults of the nave, where the Bearing of the Cross and the Crucifixion fill the large

[12] These paintings are again by several artists and present to a marked degree the same problems as the Linderöd-Bellinge group.

[13] *Danmarks Kirker* (n.2), 721 and F. Beckett, *Danmarks Kunst,* II (Copenhagen 1926) 351.

windowless wall surfaces to the north so that Elijah's sacrifice is placed just over the sacrificial death of Christ.

The paintings in the tower bay are somewhat isolated and are perhaps intended as an exhortation to imitatio Christi. In the vault there are 3 scenes from the Passion: Christ affirming his readiness to drink the cup of suffering in the garden of Gethsemane, followed by the scourging and the crowning with thorns. The last cell shows Abraham and Isaac going to the sacrifice (Fig. 5, Haastrup), Isaac with the wood on his shoulder having typologically speaking taken the cross upon himself. Down on the north wall St George fights the dragon while the king and queen look on from a large castle to the north on the west wall. On the other side of the original west door there are remains of a St Christopher. Both these saints are typical knightly saints, examples of strength, courage and endurance i.e. some of the deeds by which the Christian knight should serve God.[14] St Christopher serves the supreme lord, carrying the Infant Jesus on his shoulders. St George protects the defenceless, here a princess who is to be sacrificed to the dragon. The legend appears in a Danish folk ballad where St George serves the Virgin Mary. It is Mary who sends him out to fight the dragon, and as her knight he must decline to marry the princess.[15] The picture at Bellinge is possibly influenced by the same ideas since behind the little princess with the lamb in the foreground we see a crowned woman kneeling, larger than St George, also with a lamb on a lead (Fig. 5, Banning). Although there is no halo the giant figure is probably Mary, whose favour St George strives for in courtly manner. He has bound a large green sash around his head and around the lance a small white scarf, articles most likely belonging to the Virgin (and the princess).

The two saints in the tower vault suggest that the paintings at Bellinge may well have been donated by a nobleman. The king had an estate in Borreby in the parish.[16] The other important landowner in the locality was the Benedictine convent at Dalum, which owned 18 properties in Bellinge and received guest dues from the church.[17] The estate of the convent came under royal protection at any rate towards the end of the middle ages.[18] The lord lieutenant

---

[14] See S. Kaspersen, "Kalkmaleri og samfund 1241-1340/50", *Kulturblomstring og samfundskrise i 1300-tallet*, ed. B. Patrick McGuire (Copenhagen 1979) 133ff.

[15] *Danmarks Gamle Folkeviser*, ed. S. Grundtvig, II (Copenhagen 1856) 554-68 (nr. 103).

[16] *Danske Kancelliregistranter 1535-50*, ed. K. Erslev and W. Mollerup (Copenhagen 1881-82) 49.

[17] O. Nielsen, Dalum Klosters Jordebog 1533, *Samlinger til Fyens Historie og Topographie*, IV (1867) 308.

and the convent may have had a common interest in having the church embellished. It may be mentioned in this connection that another Funen *Biblia Pauperum* decoration from the late Gothic period was painted in Vejlby Church, which belonged to Dalum convent from 1340.[19] At Kirke-Stillinge it was possibly a descendant of the family of landed gentry at Kelstrup, who had endowed the chapel, that was resposible for the embellishment. Apparently, however, the family can only be followed to the end of the fifteenth century, i.e. to Iver Herlufsen, who is mentioned in the period 1486-93.[20] Another interested party might be the later bishop of Roskilde Lage Urne from Brostykke on Funen. While he was precentor of the cathedral chapter (1503/4-12) he altered the masses in St Anne's chapel at the church of Kirke-Stillinge,[21] which as early as 1315 had been incorporated with the newly established precentorship.[22]

With regard to the Scanian paintings we know nothing of the donors at Linderöd, but it is not unreasonable to assume that the paintings at Färlöv were undertaken at the expense of the owners of the estate of the same name, that is to say by Mouritz Nielsen Gyldenstjerne (died 1503) and his wife Margrethe Turesdatter Bjelke, or by their daughter Anne, who inherited the estate.[23] Mouritz Nielsen was one of the greatest landowners of the period. The simpler wall paintings at Östra Strö may owe their origin to the holder of the episcopal estate in the town.[24] At least a lay donor kneels beside St Thomas (Fig. 3). The church itself probably belonged to the Benedictine monastery of All Saints at Lund.[25]

The donors of these wall paintings are of the class to which such donors usually belonged in Denmark. Whether any special connection existed between the various donors of the paintings of the group is unknown, though the connection between Bellinge and Östra Strö is possibly due to the Benedictine order. However this may be, the workshop on Funen seems to have been connected with Dalum monastery. The latter also owned a good deal of

[18] Ibidem, 307.
[19] *Diplomatarium Danicum* (Copenhagen 1938ff) year 1340, no. 84.
[20] *Trap Danmark*, I-XIV (Copenhagen 1958-70[5]), III:3, 843.
[21] *Danske Magazin*, 3. rk., III, (1851) 212ff, 222, n. 15.
[22] *Diplomatarium Danicum*, year 1315, no. 294.
[23] E. Ulsig, *Danske adelsgodser i middelalderen* (Copenhagen 1968) 230-1 and 287.
[24] G. Johannesson, *Jordeböcker över Lunds ärkesätes gods vid medeltidens slut,* Skånsk senmedeltid och renässans, 7, (Lund 1953) 197-208.
[25] E. Schalling, *Kyrkogodset i Skåne, Halland och Blekinge under dansk tid* (Stockholm 1936) 131 and 247.

land in Sanderum parish[26] where the church contains wall paintings of slightly later date connected with the Bellinge group. Finally, behind the convent is perhaps another motive power, namely the king, who *may* also be responsible in some way for the lost decoration at Finderup.[27]

University of Copenhagen

[26] O. Nielsen (n.17) 308.

[27] The king owned some landed property at Kulby in the period. See *Kong Valdemars Jordebog,* ed. Sv. Aakjær I-III (Copenhagen 1926-45), I 40-18 and II 289-90.

Zur Problematik der Beziehung zwischen Bilddetail und Bildganzem

von Kurt Schier

Der Titel dieses Vortrages weist bereits darauf hin, dass die Problematik des Verhältnisses zwischen den Details eines Bildes und dem Bild als Ganzem durchaus bekannt ist und diskutiert wird. Es ist nicht meine Absicht, hier diese Problematik umfassend darzulegen oder etwa für einzelne bildliche Darstellungen neue Interpretationen zu geben; ich möchte vielmehr nur an einigen Beispielen aus dem nordischen Bereich einige der Schwierigkeiten, die sich bei der Untersuchung bildlicher Denkmäler ergeben, anschaulich machen, um zum Schluss die Frage zu stellen, ob sich nicht Wege finden lassen, diese Schwierigkeiten zu verringern. Ich lege dabei Material zugrunde, das gut bekannt und zumeist auch eingehend untersucht worden ist; manche Probleme lassen sich aber an bekannten Denkmälern wohl anschaulicher darlegen als an solchen, deren Inhalt vielen fremd ist.

Nach einleitenden Bemerkungen über die Begriffe „Bildganzes" und „Bilddetail" sollen einige dieser Fragen an drei Beispielen erörtert werden, und zwar an den Überlieferungen von Staffan Stalledräng und dem Hahnenwunder, an der isländischen Kirchentür von Valþjófsstaður sowie an einem gotländischen Bildstein von einem Grabfeld bei Smiss. Darauf folgen die bereits erwähnten Überlegungen praktischer Art.

I

Die beiden Begriffe „Bilddetail" und „Bildganzes", die ich hier in Ermangelung besserer Termini benütze, bedürfen näherer Erklärung. Vorausgeschickt sei, dass hier unter „Bild" jegliche Art von figürlicher Darstellung verstanden wird, gleichgültig ob es sich um Malerei, Steinskulptur, Schnitzerei, Metallarbeit oder um irgendeine andere Form handelt. Ornamente sollen jedoch hier nur soweit eingeschlossen sein, als sie mit figürlichen Darstellungen in Zusammenhang stehen.

Überlegt man, was die Ganzheit eines Bildes ausmacht, stösst man bald auf beträchtliche Schwierigkeiten. Am einfachsten ist das Bildganze bei in sich geschlossenen einthematischen Bildern zu fassen: es ist identisch mit dem Bild selbst. Auch Bilderreihen, wie wir sie etwa bei der Darstellung der einzelnen Stationen aus der Passion Christi oder bei einer Abfolge von Szenen aus dem Leben von Heiligen kennen, können noch leicht als ein Ganzes verstanden werden; wenn auch jedes einzelne Teilbild in sich abgeschlossen ist, fügen sich doch alle unter einen einheitlichen Gedanken, und der volle Sinn wird erst durch Zusammenschau aller Teilbilder verständlich.

Schwieriger wird es jedoch bei Bilddenkmälern, die zwar ebenfalls Teilbilder enthalten, dazu aber auch Elemente aufzuweisen haben, die nicht in eine solche Abfolge von Geschehnissen oder Szenen gehören. Ich nenne als ein Beispiel unter vielen die mittelalterlichen Taufsteine, wie sie gerade auch aus Skandinavien in reicher Zahl bezeugt sind. Sehr oft findet man bei ihnen Bilderfolgen der obengenannten Art, häufig aus der Kindheitsgeschichte Jesu, dazu aber auch – insbesondere am Fusse des Steines – Tierköpfe, Monstren und andere Figuren, und gelegentlich auch Ornamente. Wenn man nicht von vornherein annehmen will, diese Teile der Darstellung seien nur Zierat ohne Aussagewert, muss man sich bemühen, den Sinn des Ganzen zu entschlüsseln. Die einzelnen Figuren müssen dann als Bildsiglen aufgefasst werden, als Zeichen für bestimmte Vorstellungen, deren Inhalt man aber erst kennenlernen muss. Eine befriedigende Erklärung kann also nur gelingen, wenn der Code bekannt ist, und dieser Code kann in der Regel nur aus der literarischen, historischen oder philosophischen Überlieferung oder aus der theologischen Spekulation und Systematik gewonnen werden. Als bekanntes Beispiel für ein solches Bilddokument sei auf die romanische Bilddecke in der kleinen Kirche von Zillis am Südende der Via mala in der Schweiz verwiesen. Hier werden auf 105 Feldern in der Mitte Szenen und Figuren aus der Heilsgeschichte dargestellt, z.T. durchaus symbolischen Charakters; die 48 Randbilder aber zeigen Dämonen, Wasserwesen, Fabeltiere und dergleichen mehr. Die Decke stellt allem Anschein nach den Kosmos dar und spiegelt eine Vorstellung von einer in sich geordneten Welt wider.[1] Verständlich ist sie aber nur aus einer theologischen Systematik heraus.

Aber nicht bei allen aus mehreren Elementen bestehenden Bildern kann man mit Sicherheit sagen, ob sie nach einem bestimmten Grundgedanken angeordnet sind und eine Idee widerspiegeln, oder ob es sich nur um eine

---

[1] Vgl. z.B. Peter Heman [Hg.] und Ernst Murbach [Text], *Die romanische Bilderdecke in der Kirche St. Martin von Zillis*, Zürich und Freiburg i.Br. 1967.

Zusammenstellung aus zufälligen oder rein ästhetischen Gründen handelt. Die Frage, ob man es hier mit einem „Bildganzen" zu tun hat oder einer Häufung von Einzelbildern, ist dann nicht immer zu entscheiden. Es sei daran erinnert, dass dieses Problem gerade bei der Interpretation gotländischer Bildsteine auftaucht, wo es oft große Schwierigkeiten bereitet, die verschiedenen Einzelfiguren und -szenen als Glieder einer einheitlichen Vorstellung zu interpretieren.[2] Eine weitere Komplikation liegt vor, wenn die Einzelelemente selbst nicht sicher erklärbar sind. In solchen Fällen beeinflussen sich die Interpretationen der Einzelelemente und des Bildganzen oft gegenseitig.

Aber nicht nur der Begriff des Bildganzen ist schwer zu fassen, auch Bilddetails sind in ganz unterschiedlicher Weise vorstellbar. Es kann sich dabei beispielsweise um figürliche Einzelheiten handeln wie Kleidung, Haltung, Gegenstände und dergleichen mehr, oft von erheblichem kulturhistorischen Interesse. Nicht selten aber sind solche Details wiederum eine Kurzformel, eine Sigle mit bestimmter und festgelegter Bedeutung, etwa um eine Person zu charakterisieren oder zu identifizieren oder auch, um eine Handlung oder ein Geschehnis inhaltlich festzulegen. So ist z.B. der Gestus von Heiligendarstellungen in der Regel durch Überlieferung festgelegt und determiniert den Inhalt oder den Sinn eines Bildes. Ähnliches gilt für die Attribute, die ebenfalls oft als eine Art Chiffre aufzufassen sind, durch die ein bestimmter Sachverhalt in knapper, aber eindeutiger Weise festgelegt wird.

Endlich ist auch noch die Verbindung von Bilddetails zu beachten, ihr bildnerischer Kontext. Die Gruppierung gleicher Bilddetails auf verschiedenen Bildwerken weist nicht nur darauf hin, dass eine solche Zusammenstellung sinnvoll und nicht zufällig ist, sondern sie eröffnet oft auch einen Weg zur Interpretation.

II

Das erste Beispiel bezieht sich auf die Geschichte vom heiligen Stefan und dem Hahnenwunder. Da sie mehrmals untersucht worden ist, kann ich mich auf eine kurze Zusammenfassung der Fakten beschränken.[3]

---

[2] Vgl. z.B. Sune Lindqvist, *Gotlands Bildsteine. I,* Stockholm 1941, S. 104 f.; Ludwig Buisson, *Der Bildstein Ardre VIII auf Gotland,* Göttingen 1976, bes. S. 10 f. u.ö.; W. Holmqvist, in Hoops, *Reallexikon der Germanischen Altertumskunde,* 2. Auflage, Bd. 2, Berlin 1978, S. 565 u.ö.

[3] Vor allem Hilding Celander, „Staffansvisorna". In: *Folkminnen och Folktankar* 14 (1927), S. 1-55; ders., „Till Stefanslegendens och Staffansvisornas utvecklingshistoria". In: *Arv* 1 (1945), S. 1-55; Dag Strömbäck, „Kring Staffansvisan". In: *Om visor och låtar. Studier tillägn. Sven Salén,* Stockholm 1960; ders., „ St Stephen in the Ballads". In: *Arv* 24 (1968), S. 133-147.

Auf dem gotländischen Taufstein von Vänge, der von Meister Hegwald her-
rührt,[4] findet man eingefügt in eine Reihe von Bildern aus der Kindheitsgeschichte Jesu auch die Darstellung eines Königs mit einer Frau an einer
gedeckten Tafel; es muss sich um König Herodes handeln. Auf der linken
Seite steht ein Diener mit einem Gefäss in der Hand, über ihm sitzt ein grosser
Vogel, ein Hahn. Die Bedeutung der Szene ist aus ihr selbst nicht zu erkennen.
Auch gibt es keine Bibelstelle, kein apokryphes Evangelium und keine Legende in irgendeiner der grossen mittelalterlichen Legendensammlungen, die den
Schlüssel zum Verständnis der Szene bieten könnte. Ähnliche Darstellungen
finden sich aber in Skandinavien mehrmals: allein in Gotland ist sie dreimal
auf Taufsteinen bezeugt (in Vänge, Stånga und Närs), weiters auf einem Ante-
mensale aus der Kirche von Broddetorp (Västergötland), auf einem Antemen-
sale aus Løgumkloster (Amt Tønder, Jütland, ca. 1350) sowie in nicht vollstän-
diger Form auch an anderen Stellen (z.B. auf Kalkmalerien in Keldby, Møn,
ca. 1300, und Daugaard, Amt Vejle, ca. 1275; hier fehlt zwar der Hahn, die
Zugehörigkeit zu diesem Typus ist jedoch aus anderen Gründen gesichert), im
Chorumgang von Uppsala und in einem Relieffragment in der Domkirche von
Skara. Am bekanntesten und vollständigsten ist die Darstellung der Szene in
einer Deckenmalerei der Kirche von Dädesjö (Småland) vom Ende des 13.
Jahrhunderts.[6]

Die Deutung des Bildes ist jedoch leicht möglich aus späteren Balladen, die
aus Dänemark, Schweden, Finnland, von den Färöern und aus England belegt
sind.[7] Hier wird in mehreren Varianten berichtet, dass der heilige Stefan Diener oder Pferdeknecht bei König Herodes war. Bei einem Festmahl, während
er König Herodes bei Tische bedient, sieht er ein helles Licht und ruft:
„Christus natus ist!", oder er macht den König auf andere Weise auf die
Geburt Christi aufmerksam. Herodes erwidert, Christus sei ebenso wenig
geboren, als der gebratene (und manchmal schon in Stücke geschnittene)
Hahn aus der Schüssel wieder auffliegen und krähen werde. Darauf jedoch
fliegt der Hahn auf und kräht. – Die älteste skandinavische Version findet sich
in Erik Pontoppidans „Everriculum" (1736). Hier heisst es auch, dass Stefan

---

[4] Abbildung z.B. bei Uwe Lemke, *Gotland,* Stuttgart 1970, Abb. 41.

[5] Hierzu ausführlich Folke Nordström, „Virtues and Vices on the fourteenth Century Corbels
in the Choir of Uppsala Cathedral", Stockholm 1956, S. 86-93 und S. 104-106.

[6] Bengt G. Söderberg, *Mäster Sighmunder i Dädesjö,* Malmö 1957. – Marian Ullén, *Dädesjö och
Eke kyrkor* (= Sveriges kyrkor, 126), Stockholm 1969.

[7] Dag Strömbäck, in *Arv* 24 (vgl. Anm. 3). – Textbeispiele auch bei Erich Seemann, Dag Strömbäck, Bengt R. Jonsson, *European Folk Ballads,* Copenhagen 1967, S. 182-195.

sein Fohlen tränkt, und er lässt es zu Wasser „ganz bei dem hellen Sterne".[8] Auch in anderen literarischen und bildlichen Versionen (so auch in Dädesjö) wird der Stallknecht, der die Pferde wäscht, mit dem Diener des Herodes gleichgesetzt, und von daher ist eine Identifikation dieser besonderen Form der Legende ebenfalls möglich, auch wenn der Hahn selbst fehlt.

Auf die bemerkenswerte Verbindung des heiligen Stefan zu Pferden und Pferdebrauchtum sei hier nicht weiter eingegangen; zu beachten ist immerhin, dass auch heute noch an zahlreichen Orten in Süddeutschland am Tag des heiligen Stefan (26. Dezember) Umritte um die Kirche stattfinden, zumeist verbunden mit einer Segnung der Pferde.[9] Auch bleibe die Frage hier unerörtert, weshalb der Erzmärtyrer Stefan, der nach der Apostelgeschichte Kap. 6-7 ein Angehöriger der christlichen Urgemeinde in Jerusalem war und als erster von allen Anhängern Christi gesteinigt wurde und den Märtyrertod erlitt, in diesen Balladen Knecht bei König Herodes sein soll. Über diese Fragen ist viel geschrieben worden, wenn auch das Thema wohl noch nicht ganz geklärt ist.[10]

Für unsere Überlegungen ist die Überlieferung von Sankt Stefan jedoch vor allem aus drei Gründen von Bedeutung:

1) Die bildliche Darstellung, *und nur sie allein,* bezeugt die Existenz dieses Stoffes in Dänemark und Schweden runde 500 Jahre vor dem ersten schriftlichen Beleg und ermöglicht so wichtige Schlüsse auf die Stofftradition. Dies ist besonders bedeutsam, weil die Stefans-Überlieferungen in dieser Art auf dem Kontinent nicht nachzuweisen sind, das Hahnenwunder allein zwar bezeugt ist, aber nur in Verbindung mit anderen Heiligen (etwa dem hl. Jakobus).

2) Die Interpretation der bildlichen Darstellungen beruht ausschliesslich auf den späteren Balladen. Hätten wir sie nicht, bliebe der Sinn des Bildes wohl dunkel.

3) Das Bild wird jeweils *nur durch ein einziges Detail gekennzeichnet,* nämlich den Hahn auf dem Tisch oder – worauf oben nicht näher eingegangen werden konnte[11] – bei den Bildern mit Stefan als Pferdetränker durch das Bild eines Sternes mit seinem Spiegelbild im Wasser.

Die Möglichkeit der wechselseitigen Erhellung der bildlichen durch die lite-

---

[8] *Danmarks gamle Folkeviser,* II. Del, Kjøbenhavn 1856, S. 525 (= DgF 96). Vgl. auch *DgF* III, S. 883-885 und *DgF* X, S. 194-198.

[9] Seit 1945 hat dieser Brauch wieder stark zugenommen.

[10] Zusammenfassend dazu Dag Strömbäck, „Staffan", In *KLNM* XVII, 1972, Sp. 23-27.

[11] Dazu besonders Folke Nordström, „Virtues and Vices" (s. Anm. 5), bes. S. 86-93, sowie Dag Strömbäck, „Kring Staffansvisan", (s. Anm. 3).

rarische und der literarischen durch die bildliche Überlieferung liegt hier ebenso klar zutage wie die außerordentliche Wichtigkeit einzelner Bilddetails. Dabei ist zu bedenken, dass die Voraussetzungen für die Bewahrung von Überlieferungen innerhalb christlich-religiöser Texte von vornherein sehr viel günstiger sind als die profaner oder gar heidnisch-religiöser Vorstellungen.

III

Das wohl bekannteste isländische Schnitzwerk des Mittelalters ist die Tür von Valþjófsstaður, die nun in Þjóðminjasafn in Reykjavík verwahrt ist.[12] Diese Tür, die nicht vor der Mitte des 12. Jahrhunderts, möglicherweise aber erst etwa zwischen 1200 und 1230 entstanden ist, zeigt zwei grosse, übereinander angeordnete Kreise. Der untere enthält einen geflügelten Drachen, der sich in seinen Schweif beisst. Der Drache wird viermal abgebildet, jeweils um 90° gedreht, so dass Leib, Gliedmassen und Flügel des Drachen kunstvoll zu einem Ornament ineinander verschlungen sind. – Der obere Kreis ist in zwei Hälften geteilt. Das untere Feld zeigt einen Löwen im Kampf mit einem geflügelten Drachen. Ein Ritter reitet heran und durchbohrt mit seinem Schwert den Drachen. Der lässt sein Opfer, den Löwen, den er schon umschlungen hatte, im Todeskampf frei. Rechts oben sieht man drei Tierköpfe – vielleicht die Jungen des Löwen. Über dem Pferd des Ritters fliegt ein Vogel. – Die obere Hälfte dieses Kreises besteht offenbar aus einer Aufeinanderfolge von zwei Szenen. In der Mitte sieht man wiederum den Ritter mit Schwert und Schild, gefolgt von einem Löwen. Auf der Mähne des Pferdes sitzt ein Vogel, wohl ein Jagdfalke. Auf der rechten Seite des Bildes liegt auf einem Grabstein, der eine Runeninschrift trägt, ein ganz abgemagerter Löwe, zu seinen Häupten ein Kreuz. Die Runeninschrift spricht von einem König, der hier begraben ist. – Aus bekannten Motivparallelen lässt sich der Gang der Geschichte erschliessen: Ein Ritter kommt dazu, wie ein Drache mit einem Löwen kämpft und ihn zu besiegen droht; er tötet den Drachen und befreit so den Löwen, der folgt ihm von nun an. Als der Ritter stirbt und begraben ist, ruht der Löwe auf seinem Grab, verweigert das Essen und magert ab, bis er – so berichten manche Versionen der Geschichte – auf dem Grab des Ritters stirbt.

[12] Vgl. etwa Anders Bæksted, *Islands Runeindskrifter*. (= Bibl. Arnamagn.Vol. II), København 1942. S. 181-200, Tafeln 92-95. Gute Abbildungen des oberen Bildkreises z.B. bei Kristján Eldjárn, *Alte isländische Kunst*, München 1957, Tafel 13, sowie bei Kristján Eldjárn, *Hundrað ár í Þjóðminjasafni*, Reykjavík ³1969, S. 68.

Die Schwierigkeit bei der Interpretation des Bildes liegt in erster Linie darin, dass es zwar einige literarische Überlieferungen gibt, die in mehreren Punkten dem Bild entsprechen, jedoch keine aus dem Norden, die sich ganz mit dessen Inhalt deckt. Als Vergleichstext angeführt wurde u.a. die Sage von Dietrichs von Bern Kampf mit dem Drachen, doch weiss diese Geschichte nichts davon, dass der Löwe dem König folgt. In der *Ívens saga*, Kap. 10, sowie in der *Vilhjálms saga sjóðs*, Kap. 8, wird zwar ebenfalls von einem entsprechenden Kampf berichtet, und hier wird sogar erzählt, dass der Löwe dem Ritter folgte, aber man findet keinen Hinweis darauf, dass er auf seines Herrn Grab lag und dort sein Ende fand.[13] Andererseits ist eben das Ende des treuen Löwen auf dem Grab seines Herrn ein in der Volksüberlieferung nicht selten bezeugtes Motiv; im Typenverzeichnis von Aarne und Thompson ist es unter der Nummer AT 156 A verzeichnet, Belege werden vor allem aus dem slawischen und baltischen Bereich angeführt.[14] Wenn Anders Bæksted meinte, dass das Ende des Löwen auf dem Grabe vielleicht Erfindung des Schnitzers sei,[15] so widerspricht dem bereits die Tatsache, dass dieses Motiv auch anderswo bezeugt ist. Vor allem aber findet man im Zusammenhang mit Sagen über den Braunschweiger Herzog Heinrich den Löwen unter anderen Abenteuern auch gerade die Motivkombination, die auf der Tür von Valþjófsstaður vorzuliegen scheint: Hilfe eines Ritters für einen Löwen bei dessen Kampf mit einem Drachen, Gefolgschaft des Löwen, Tod des treuen Löwen auf des Ritters Grab.[16] Hermann Schneider hatte auch schon als älteste Form dieser Überlieferung eine Ballade postuliert, die noch vor 1200 angesetzt werden müsste und die alle diese Motive enthielt.[17] Ein wichtiges Argument für Schneiders Hypothese bildete gerade die Darstellung auf der Tür von Valþjófsstaður. Aber die Postulierung einer Ballade über den Heinrich-den-Löwen-Stoff in so früher Zeit stösst auf erhebliche Schwierigkeiten verschiedener, nicht zuletzt chrono-

[13] *Ívens saga*, hg. von Eugen Kölbing, Halle 1898 (= Altnord. Saga-Bibliothek, Heft 7), Kap. 10, bes. S. 75-78. – *Vilhjálms saga sjóðs*, In: *Late Medieval Icelandic Romances*, ed. by Agnete Loth, Copenhagen 1964 (= Edit. Arnamagn., Ser. B., Vol. 23), bes. S. 26 f.

[14] Antti Aarne [and] Stith Thompson, *The Types of the Folktale*, Second Revision. Helsinki 1961 (= *FFC* No. 184), S. 57.

[15] A. Bæksted, *Islands Runeindskrifter* (s. Anm. 12), S. 192.

[16] Vgl. hierzu jetzt vor allem Helge Gerndt, „Das Nachleben Heinrichs des Löwen in der Sage", In: Wolf-Dieter Mohrmann [Hg.], *Heinrich der Löwe*, Göttingen 1980. S. 440-465. (Im Druck) – Ich danke Herrn Kollegen Gerndt für die Freundlichkeit, mir seine Arbeit bereits im Manuskript zugänglich gemacht zu haben.

[17] Hermann Schneider, „Ursprung und Alter der deutschen Volksballade", In: *Vom Werden des deutschen Geistes*, Festschrift für Gustav Ehrismann, 1925. S. 112-124, bes. S. 118.

logischer Art. Darüber hinaus bleiben auch damit manche Einzelheiten unge-
klärt, einige Details – z.b. die Runeninschrift, die von einem „König" spricht –
stehen in direktem Widerspruch zur deutschen Überlieferung. Eine einiger-
massen gesicherte Textgrundlage bietet erst eine Ballade von 98 Strophen mit
dem Titel „Eyn buoch von dem edeln hern von Bruneczwigk, als er über mer
fûre", die in einer Handschrift aus dem Jahre 1474 erhalten ist.[18] Hier findet
man tatsächlich die wichtigsten der Motive vereint, die wir von der isländischen Tür kennen. Natürlich ist dieser Text viel zu spät, um unmittelbar als
Interpretationshilfe für die Tür dienen zu können; er zeigt aber immerhin, dass
der Teil des Bildes, der den Löwen auf des Ritters Grab ruhend darstellt, ent-
gegen der Auffassung von Bæksted nicht Erfindung des Schnitzers sein kann.
Die Frage bleibt offen, welcher literarische Text die Grundlage für die Schnitzerei gebildet hat. Unerklärbare Details schliessen also eine Reihe von Interpretationen aus. Wie bei den Hahnenwunder-Darstellungen hat auch hier die
Chronologie eine sehr grosse Bedeutung. Man wird also nach Möglichkeiten
suchen müssen, wonach auch in früher Zeit eine derartige Motivkombination
für Island anzusetzen ist. In diesem Zusammenhang wird vielleicht sogar die
antike Tradition überprüft werden müssen; es ist ja bekannt, dass das Motiv
des dankbaren Löwen auch in den Gesta Romanorum in der Androklus-
Geschichte weit bekannt war.[19]

IV

Im Jahre 1955 berichtete Sune Lindqvist, der Altmeister der Erforschung der
gotländischen Bildsteine, über einen neugefundenen Bildstein aus Smiss, När
socken.[20] Es ist ein Stein der Gruppe A (stehende senkrechte Platten mit einer
bogenförmigen Oberkante); diese Steine sind in der Regel besonders gut bear-
beitet. Der Stein von Smiss müsste etwa in das 5. Jahrhundert gesetzt werden.
Er ist oben und an der Seite von einer Flechtbandborte umgeben. In der oberen Hälfte des Bildfeldes findet man einen dreigliedrigen Flechtknoten, dessen
einzelne Glieder in drei verschiedene Tierköpfe auslaufen. Nach Lindqvist
handelt es sich um ein Wildschwein, einen Adler und möglicherweise um

[18] W. Seehaussen, *Michel Wyssenherres Gedicht „Von dem edeln hern von Bruneczwigk, als er über
mer fure"* und die Sage von Heinrich dem Löwen, 1913. (Germanist. Abhandlingen 43), bes. S. 73
ff.

[19] Vgl. AT 156 (s. Anm. 14) mit weiteren Hinweisen.

[20] Sune Lindqvist, „Tre nyfunna bildstenar", In: *Gotländskt Arkiv* 27 (1955), S. 41 – 52, über
den Bildstein von Smiss S. 42-48.

einen Wolf – eine Zusammenstellung, die auch sonst belegt ist, insbesondere auf dem Kontinent und hier vor allem bei den Franken. Unter diesem Knoten sieht man eine menschliche Figur mit weit gespreizten Beinen, die frontal dargestellt wird; es ist nicht sicher, ob die Gestalt als sitzend aufzufassen ist. Vom Kopf führen zwei (Haar-?) Stränge waagerecht nach aussen weg, bilden dann jeweils eine Art Knoten und hängen an den Enden weit nach unten. Die Arme der Gestalt sind nach aussen abgewinkelt, jede Hand fasst eine dicke gewundene Schlange. Nach Lindqvist ist die Gestalt am ehesten als eine nackte oder mit ganz eng anliegender Kleidung versehene Frau aufzufassen.

Genaue Parallelen zu dieser streng stilisierten Komposition fehlen. Lindqvist suchte nach einer Erklärung des Bildes auf zwei verschiedenen Wegen und bemühte sich zunächst, ältere Vorbilder zu finden.[21] Man könnte z.b. an die kretische „Schlangengöttin" erinnern, eine bronzezeitliche Fayence-Plastik, bei der allerdings die Göttin aufrecht steht und mit einem langen drapierten Rock bekleidet ist. Auch wenn man andere Darstellungen zum Vergleich heranzieht, die näher am Fundplatz des Bildsteines liegen, werden die Parallelen nicht überzeugender; bei dem aus ostkeltischem Umkreis stammenden Silberkessel von Gundestrup ist zu beachten, dass Männer und Frauen, die hier auf Brustbildern dargestellt sind, in den ausgestreckten Händen Menschen oder Tiere halten, doch niemals Schlangen.

Nähere Übereinstimmungen meinte Lindqvist dann erst auf erheblich jüngeren Bildwerken zu finden,[22] z.B. in Darstellungen, auf denen sich ein Mann gegen angreifende Schlangen verteidigt, etwa auf einer Bildsteinkiste von Ardre (11. Jahrhundert), auf einer Runenritzung von Aspö in Södermanland, auf Schnitzereien aus dem Osebergwagen sowie auf einem Bronzeschmuck aus Bornholm (Ende 8. Jahrhundert), um nur einige Funde zu nennen. Aber fast alle diese Bilder vermitteln einen ganz anderen Eindruck als die „posierende Göttergestalt" auf dem Stein von Smiss. – Dagegen sieht Lindqvist deutliche Parallelen zu Darstellungen an romanischen Kirchen, bei denen man öfter das Bild einer Frau findet, an deren nackten Brüsten Schlangen hängen. In der Regel wird dies als Abbild der Unkeuschheit, als Luxuria aufgefasst (was allerdings nicht immer ganz überzeugend scheint). Gerade auf Gotland, in Väte,[23] findet man ein Kalksteinrelief aus dem 12. Jahrhundert, auf dem zwei geflügelte Drachen an den Brüsten einer Frau saugen, während in ihren Achselhöhlen ein Frosch und eine Schlange hängen.

[21] Lindqvist, a.a.O., S. 44 f.
[22] Lindqvist, a.a.O., S 45 ff.
[23] Abbildung bei Lindqvist, a.a.O., S. 47.

Nun kan man sicher nicht mit einem direkten Zusammenhang zwischen Bildern rechnen, die zeitlich so weit auseinanderliegen und so verschiedene Funktion besitzen und noch dazu aus so unterschiedlichen kulturellen und religiösen Vorstellungswelten stammen. Lindqvist rechnet aber damit, dass in solchen christlichen religiösen Bildern eine Figur aus der keltischen Götterwelt eine ganz neue Funktion erhalten hat. Diese Gestalt sei nun nicht mehr Beherrscherin der Tiere, sondern sie habe sich gegen ihr Hauen und Beissen zu wehren.[24]

Unter dem Aspekt der Relation zwischen Bildganzem und Bilddetail ist diese Interpretation in mehrfacher Weise interessant.

1) Für unsere anfängliche Überlegung, was ein „Bild" als Ganzes eigentlich ist, liegt hier ein gutes Beispiel vor. Beide Bildelemente, der Flechtknoten mit den drei Tierköpfen und die Figur mit den beiden Schlangen in den Händen scheinen Teile eines Bildes zu sein und sollten deshalb aufeinander bezogen und gemeinsam interpretiert werden.

2) Trotz der Form der beiden Haarstränge kann es nicht als sicher gelten, dass es sich bei dieser Figur tatsächlich um eine Frau handelt. Holzapfel[25] wie auch Wilhelm Holmqvist[26] lassen diese Frage offen, Karl Hauck dagegen[27] fasst die Gestalt als Mann auf, beschäftigt sich aber auch eingehend mit der Frage des Geschlechtes der Figur. Gerade dieses Problem kann aber von entscheidender Bedeutung für die Interpretation des Bildes sein.

3) Prinzipiell wichtig ist jedoch die Frage, ob die Darstellung einer Frau mit Schlangen an den Brüsten überhaupt vergleichbar ist der Figur auf dem Bildstein von Smiss. Worin liegt denn eigentlich das Vergleichbare? Gemeinsam ist beiden Darstellungen nur eine menschliche Figur und zwei schlangenförmigen Wesen. Der Gestus der Figur von Smiss mit den Schlangen in den Händen ist grundverschieden von dem einer Frau mit Schlangen an den Brüsten. Solange keine Klarheit über die Bedeutung der beiden Darstellungen besteht, kann man vorerst nur die Übereinstimmungen, aber auch die Unterschiede der beiden Bilder konstatieren.

Auch wenn man im Bereich der romanischen Skulptur bleibt, könnte das Vergleichsmaterial bei genauerem Suchen noch erheblich erweitert werden. So zeigt ein Kapitell im Chor einer Kirche von Solignac (Limousin, Frank-

---

[24] Lindqvist, a.a.O., S. 48.

[25] Otto Holzapfel, „Stabilität und Variabilität einer Formel", In: *Mediaeval Scandinavia* 6 (1973), S. 7-38, hier S. 30, wo er von einer „Figur" zwischen Schlangen spricht.

[26] Wilhelm Holmqvist, in Hoops, *Reallexikon* (s. Anm. 2), Bd. 2, S. 562.

[27] Karl Hauck, *Goldbrakteaten aus Sievern,* München 1970. Bes. S. 152-156 sowie S. 281.

reich)[28] eine menschliche Figur, anscheinend einen Mann, der mit weit aus-
einandergestellten Beinen dasteht; der Körper wird frontal, Arme und Beine
werden beinahe im Profil dargestellt. Die Arme sind nach der Seite gestreckt,
mit jeder Hand umfasst die Gestalt eine Schlange, deren Schwanz zu einem
lockeren Knoten geschlungen ist. Obwohl auch diese Figur noch keineswegs
mit der Gestalt auf dem gotländischen Stein in allen Details übereinstimmt,
besteht doch eine viel stärkere Ähnlichkeit zwischen beiden Bildwerken als
mit den sogenannten Luxuria-Darstellungen. Vergleichbare Beispiele gibt es
aber, wie es scheint, noch in grösserer Anzahl, und die eigentliche Schwierigkeit in der Interpretation dürfte darin zu suchen sein, in welchem Umfang Vergleichsmaterial herangezogen wird, und wieweit man nur in Teilen überein-
stimmende Elemente als noch vergleichbar betrachtet.

Es sei auch nur am Rande erwähnt, dass der Sinn der sogenannten Luxuria-Darstellungen keineswegs immer gesichert ist. In der antiken Überlieferung gelten Schlangen oft als die Tiere der Erde, und eine weibliche Gestalt,
die Schlangen nährt, dürfte mehrmals als eine Darstellung des Elementes Erde
aufzufassen sein. Es ist zu fragen, wieweit sich derartige Vorstellungen auch
noch in den romanischen Bildwerken widerspiegeln. Nimmt man dies an,
ergäben sich für die Erklärung des Bildes von Smiss auch mit diesem Vergleichsmaterial viel weitere Möglichkeiten.

Auch Wilhelm Holmqvist widmete dem Stein von Smiss seine Aufmerk-
samkeit.[29] Er zog aber ganz andere Vergleichsbilder heran, nämlich Nach-
prägungen byzantinischer Goldsolidi, die auf Gotland gefunden wurden. Eine
menschliche Figur auf diesen Solidi zeigt eine ganz ähnliche Beinstellung wie
die Gestalt auf dem Bildstein, und auch die schlangenartigen Drachen finden
sich hier, allerdings zwischen den Beinen des Mannes.

Ganz andere Wege bei der Interpretation des Steines von Smiss schlug Karl
Hauck ein. In seiner grossen Untersuchung „Gold aus Sievern"[30] verwies er
auf eine Abhandlung von A. Alföldy, die sich mit einer aus dem 13. Jahrhundert v. Chr. stammenden Votivbronze aus Luristan beschäftigte.[31] Diese
Bronze zeigt nach Alföldy ein nacktes knieendes „Urwesen", das in den

---

[28] Abbildung z.B. bei Ingeborg Tetzlaff, *Romanische Kapitelle in Frankreich,* Köln 1976, Abb. 35.

[29] Hoops, Reallexikon (s. Anm. 2), Bd. 2, S. 562. – Vgl. auch Birgit Arrhenius och Wilhelm
Holmqvist, „En bildsten revideras", In: *Fornvännen* 55 (1960), S. 173-192.

[30] Vgl. Anm. 27.

[31] Hauck, *Goldbrakteaten aus Sievern,* S. 154; Andreas Alföldy, „Der iranische Weltriese auf
archäologischen Denkmälern", In: *Jahrbuch der Schweizerischen Gesellschaft für Urgeschichte* 40
(1949/50), S. 17 ff.

Händen zwei sich nach oben bewegende Schlangen hält. Die Gestalt hat einen Bart, besitzt aber auch Brüste und ist wohl als Zwitter aufzufassen.[32] Alföldy sieht in ihm ein androgynes Urwesen, das die beiden Stammeltern der Menschen in Schlangengestalt in den Händen hält. Die kosmogonische Vorstellung von einem zweigeschlechtlichen Urwesen ist auch dem Norden nicht fremd, und Ymir kann wohl mit Recht in diesen Umkreis einbezogen werden.

Karl Hauck verwies in diesem Zusammenhang auf die *Guta saga,* eine Einleitung zum *Gutalag,* dem alten Rechtsbuch der Insel Gotland. Die *Guta saga* enthält einen kurzen Bericht über die sagenhafte erste Besiedlung der Insel, und es wurde schon vor langer Zeit – vor allem von Franz Rolf Schröder[33] – angenommen, dass es sich bei diesem Bericht um einen kosmogonischen Mythos handelt. Hier heisst es, dass Gotland zuerst von einem Mann namens Thielvar gefunden worden sei, und es sei tags untergesunken und nachts oben gewesen. Thielvar aber brachte Feuer ans Land, und seitdem sank es niemals. Thielvar hatte einen Sohn Hafthi, und sein Weib hiess Huita-Stierna, die bauten sich zuerst in Gotland an. ,,Die erste Nacht, als sie zusammen schliefen, da träumte ihr ein Traum, als wenn drei Schlangen zusammen geschlungen wären in ihrem Busen, und deuchte ihr, als wenn sie aus ihrem Busen kröchen. Diesen Traum erzählte sie Hafthi, ihrem Mann, er deutete den Traum also: Alles ist befestigt; – bewohntes Land wird dies werden und wir werden drei Söhne haben – denen allen gab er Namen ungeboren: Guti wird Gotland besitzen, Graipr wird der andere heissen und Gunnfiaun der dritte. Diese teilten dann Gotland in drei Dritteile...''[34]

Thielvar dürfte – wie schon Franz Rolf Schröder gezeigt hat – tatsächlich ein androgynes Urwesen sein. Seine Abkömmlinge sind das erste Paar und nach Auffassung Haucks in Schlangengestalt vorzustellen. Unter Heranziehung eines umfangreichen Vergleichsmaterials, vor allem aus dem mediterranen Bereich, kommt Hauck zu dem Schluss, dass für die Urmenschenvorstellung nicht nur das doppelte Geschlecht, sondern auch die Schlangen als signifikantes Detail gelten.[35]

Der Stein von Smiss enthält also – wenn diese Auffassung richtig ist – eine Darstellung eines androgynen Urwesens, das das schlangengestaltige Ureltern-

---

[32] Abbildung bei Karl Hauck, *Goldbrakteaten aus Sievern,* Abb. 17,1 und 17,2.

[33] Franz Rolf Schröder, ,,Die Göttin des Urmeeres und ihr männlicher Partner'', In: *Beiträge zur Geschichte der deutschen Sprache und Literatur* 82 (1960), bes. S. 232 f.

[34] *Gutalag och Gutasaga,* utg. af Hugo Pipping, København 1905-07. S. 62. – Übersetzung nach Hauck, *Goldbrakteaten aus Sievern,* S. 153.

[35] Hauck, a.a.O., S. 155.

paar in Händen hält. Es spricht kaum etwas dagegen, wenn man dann die drei miteinander verflochtenen Schlangen mit verschiedenen Tierköpfen in der oberen Bildhälfte in Beziehung setzt zu den drei Söhnen, die nach der *Guta saga* der Huita-Stierna in Schlangengestalt aus dem Busen kriechen. Auf diese Weise fände nicht nur ein Teil des Bildes eine Erklärung, sondern die ganze Darstellung, und die Interpretation könnte sich auf eine einheimische Überlieferung stützen.

Wenn auch diese Deutung sehr viel für sich hat und erhebliche Konsequenzen für die Interpretation von Bildsteinen überhaupt besitzt, so geht es mir in diesem Zusammenhang jedoch gar nicht so sehr um eine Bilderklärung im einzelnen. Für unsere Frage ist es aber höchst aufschlussreich zu sehen, wie drei so angesehene Forscher wie Sune Lindqvist, Wilhelm Holmqvist und Karl Hauck bei der Interpretation des gleichen Bildwerkes zu so überaus unterschiedlichen Ergebnissen kommen. Die Differenzen sind allem Anschein nach vor allem auf zwei Tatsachen zurückzuführen: erstens werden von manchen Forschern Details als signifikant betrachtet, die anderen bereits als zu allgemein und nicht mehr signifikant gelten. Darauf wurde bereits oben im Zusammenhang mit der Interpretation von Sune Lindqvist hingewiesen. – Zum zweiten aber wird von jedem der drei Forscher ganz unterschiedliches Vergleichsmaterial herangezogen, wobei sicher nicht von vornherein behauptet werden kann, diese oder jene Vergleichsbilder seien als nicht signifikant unverwendbar. Bei der weiten Verbreitung von Bildchiffren und der Zähigkeit, mit der Bildelemente erhalten bleiben können, auch wenn sich ihre Bedeutung beim Wechsel in einen anderen Vorstellungsumkreis ändert, kann man in der Regel weder räumlich weit entferntes noch zeitlich sehr viel jüngeres oder älteres Material ohne weiteres ausschliessen. Natürlich bleibt als Postulat bestehen, dass zunächst Vergleichsmaterial herangezogen werden muss, das zeitlich und räumlich dem untersuchten Bildwerk nahe steht und auch den gleichen kulturellen und religiösen Quellen entspringt wie dieses.

V

Ein – vorerst freilich utopisch erscheinender – Ausweg aus diesem Dilemma bestünde in einer möglichst vollständigen und zuverlässigen Sammlung des Materials. Das Fehlen solcher Hilfsmittel wurde schon mehrmals beklagt. So wies z.B. Emil Ploss bereits vor vielen Jahren darauf hin, dass ein Corpus der

Bilddarstellungen zur Heldensage ein dringendes Desiderat sei.[36] Karl Hauck
stellte vor allem folgende Probleme heraus:[37]

1) Eine kritische Überprüfung der Originale sei erforderlich. Hauck selbst
hatte verschiedentlich bereits durch verfeinerte Methoden der Untersuchung
und der Bildwiedergabe neue Ergebnisse erzielen können.

2) Es bestehen noch grosse Editionslücken. Nur wenige Gruppen von Bilddenkmälern liegen in guten kritischen Editionen vor.

3) In der Literatur erscheinen die wenigen bedeutenden Denkmäler oft iso-
liert, da die Denkmäler von geringerer künstlerischer Bedeutung, die aber für
die Ikonologie nicht weniger wichtig sind, oft nicht ediert wurden.

4) Der bildnerische Kontext muss erfasst und berücksichtigt werden.

Hinzuzufügen ist, dass die Publikation von Bildern vor allem in älteren Aus-
gaben oft unter der mangelnden technischen Qualität der Wiedergabe leidet,
so dass Einzelheiten, die für eine Analyse wichtig sind, zuweilen nur unzuläng-
lich wiedergegeben werden.

Geht man einmal davon aus, dass das gesamte Bildmaterial des Nordens
innerhalb eines umgrenzten, aber doch grossen Zeitraumes auf diese Weise
erfasst werden sollte, ohne Rücksicht auf die künstlerische Qualität der Bilddenkmäler, so erscheint es hoffnungslos, auf entsprechende Editionen zu
warten, die wohl wegen des Arbeitsaufwandes und der erheblichen Kosten
nur zu einem geringen Teil in absehbarer Zeit realisierbar sein dürften. Für
den Forscher, der ikonographische und ikonologische Probleme aufgrund
eines wirklich umfassenden Materials bearbeiten möchte, oder gar für den
Literaturwissenschaftler oder Folkloristen, der die schriftliche oder orale
Überlieferung im Zusammenhang mit den Bildtraditionen sehen möchte, ist
damit wenig getan. Ein praktikabler Ausweg, durch den sowohl dem ver-
gleichend arbeitenden Forscher Vergleichsmöglichkeiten in absehbarer Zeit
gegeben als auch Voraussetzungen für spätere kritische Editionen geschaffen
würden, könnte vielleicht in der Errichtung eines umfassenden Bildarchivs
liegen. Es gibt zweifellos zahlreiche Museen, Institute und Archive, die über
reiches Bildmaterial verfügen, doch ist es für viele Aufgaben nicht nur überaus
mühselig, sich das Vergleichsmaterial an vielen verstreuten Stellen zusammen-
zusuchen, sondern oft ganz unmöglich, weil man nur sucht, wo man von vornherein weiss oder annimmt, dass dort bestimmte Bildwerke vorhanden sind.

Ein solches Archiv sollte folgende Aufgaben haben:

---

[36] Emil Ploss, *Siegfried-Sigurd, der Drachenkämpfer*, Köln, Graz 1966. S. 119.

[37] Karl Hauck, in Hoops, *Reallexikon der German. Altertumskunde* (s. Anm. 2), Bd. 2, S. 578 f.

1) Schrittweise systematische Sammlung von technisch einwandfreien Fotos in ausreichendem Format von allen Bilddenkmälern innerhalb eines noch zu umgrenzenden räumlichen und zeitlichen Rahmens.

2) Ordnung und Katalogisierung der Bilddenkmäler.

3) Schaffung eines ikonographischen Index.

4) Eventuell Erarbeitung einer Bibliographie der Bilddenkmäler.

Diese Sammlung sollte allen interessierten Forschern zur Verfügung stehen. Eine ideale Lösung bestünde darin, ein solches Archiv parallel an verschiedenen Stellen zu haben, etwa je eines in den einzelnen skandinavischen Ländern, in Grossbritannien und in Deutschland. Wenn ein solches Unternehmen als Gemeinschaftsarbeit verschiedener Forscher und Institutionen in mehreren Ländern organisiert würde, so könnte an verschiedenen Orten gearbeitet werden, die Ergebnisse aber allen anderen Arbeitsstellen zugänglich gemacht werden. Die Voraussetzung ist allerdings, dass die Prinzipien, die der Beschaffung des Materials, der technischen Verarbeitung, der Ordnung und Katalogisierung und dergleichen zugrundeliegen, an allen Arbeitsstellen gleich sind. Die Mehrkosten, die dadurch entstehen, dass jedes Bilddokument nicht einmal, sondern beispielsweise fünfmal erstellt wird, dürften durch die weit grösseren und besseren praktischen Arbeitsmöglichkeiten reichlich aufgewogen werden. Die Anlage eines solchen Archives an mehreren Orten nebeneinander ist nicht ganz ohne Beispiel; so hat etwa die Arbeitsstelle der „ Enzyklopädie des Märchens" in Göttingen einschlägige Archivbestände ausländischer Erzählarchive systematisch kopiert. Es wäre auch zu überlegen, ob bei einer derartigen internationalen Zusammenarbeit die Finanzierungsmöglichkeiten nicht günstiger wären als bei einem nationalen Projekt.

Besonders wichtig erscheint mir die Schaffung eines ikonographischen Index, da nur auf diese Weise das Material wirklich ganz erschlossen werden kann. Dies ist zweifellos ein besonders schwieriges Unterfangen, aber es dürfte nach einigen Vorarbeiten und Versuchen lösbar sein. Die Voraussetzung dürfte darin bestehen, ein System einer genauen Bildbeschreibung zu entwickeln, durch die alle Bildelemente erfasst werden können. Auch diese Arbeit ist keineswegs ohne Vorbild; schon an anderer Stelle habe ich einmal auf die Arbeit des „Instituts für mittelalterliche Realienkunde Österreichs" der Österreichischen Akademie der Wissenschaften in Krems verwiesen.[38] Hier wird

---

[38] Kurt Schier, „Einige methodische Überlegungen zum Problem vom mündlicher und literarischer Tradition im Norden", In: *Oral Tradition – Literary Tradition,* Odense 1977. S. 98-115, hier S. 115.

seit einem runden Jahrzehnt mit guten Erfolgen der Versuch gemacht, das gesamte Bildmaterial der österreichischen Tafelmalerei zu sammeln, in technisch guten Fotografien zu archivieren und es durch ein Beschreibungssystem zugänglich zu machen. Zu diesem Zweck wurde bereits vor Jahren ein Computersystem entwickelt, mit dessen Hilfe es möglich ist, nicht nur alle Details und Bildinhalte rasch für eine vergleichende Untersuchung bereitzustellen, sondern auch Fragen des bildnerischen Kontextes, der geographischen und zeitlichen Streuung von Bildern oder Bildelementen und viele andere Fragen zu beantworten.

Dieser Vorschlag, ein überregionales oder internationales Archiv der Bilddenkmäler des Nordens zum Nutzen aller an diesen Fragen interessierten Forscher zu schaffen, mag jetzt als eine nie realisierbare Utopie erscheinen. Es ist auch ganz sicher, dass hierfür zahlreiche Probleme zu klären wären, nicht zuletzt organisatorische, rechtliche und finanzielle. Trotzdem sei dieser Plan hier in aller Kürze zur Diskussion gestellt.

Universität München

The Vǫlsung legend in medieval art

by SUE MARGESON

The Vǫlsung legend is, to say the least, well known and its iconography undoubtedly familiar. It is in fact so familiar after the exhibition at the Old-saksamling in Oslo in 1972-3, and the subsequent proliferation of articles on the subject by Scandinavian, German and British scholars,[1] that you may well ask "Why Sigurðr yet again?"

This paper should be sub-titled "Sigurðr: a suitable case for treatment" because I believe that a critical re-assessment of this material is long overdue. It is in fact because the corpus has been known for so long – since the mid-nineteenth century to be precise – that some identifications have gained credence which barely stand up to critical examination. Rather than discovering new Vǫlsung illustrations, the intention of my research has been to investigate the corpus systematically in order to weed out the dubious material and to formulate criteria for reliable identification of the Vǫlsung iconography.

As a salutary lesson to remind us of the difficulties in identifying much of this pictorial material of a secular or profane character, let us consider for a moment the Sutton Hoo purse-lid of the seventh century and a twelfth-century tapestry from Skog in Hälsingland in Sweden, both of which have representations of Óðinn – or so we have been told.

The 'Óðinn' on the Sutton Hoo purse-lid is based on the claim that one of the figures between two boars is one-eyed; but that is a misconception for the apparent closing of one eye was in fact due to a blob of conservator's resin. The figure is undoubtedly two-eyed, both eyes having originally been set with garnet, like the other figure between two boars on the purse-lid.

The Skog tapestry has three standing figures shown outside a church, the figures often identified as Óðinn, Þórr and Freyr. The identification of the tri-

---

[1] M. Blindheim and E. Hohler, *Sigurds saga i middelalderens billedkunst* (1972-3), catalogue of the exhibition; M. Blindheim, "Fra hedensk sagnfigur til kristent forbilde", *Den Iconographiske Post* (1973 pt. 3), 2-28; E. Hohler, "Sigurd og valkyrien på Hindarfjell", *Den Iconographiske Post* (1973 pt. 3), 29-38. See also many other articles on the subject in ICO.

umvirate of gods depends solely on the identification of Óðinn the one-eyed. However, detailed research by Franzén has shown that though the thread has now disappeared, there are stitch-marks in the position of the second eye.[2]

We thus approach the Vǫlsung iconography with due circumspection! Well-defined Vǫlsung illustrations occur in the late Viking Age for the first time. Here the scenes are represented without episodic divisions, unlike the illustrations of the twelfth and thirteenth centuries where separate episodes are often contained in medallions. Within each chronological group, diagnostic features have to be isolated which are compatible with the different methods of narrative illustration. Nevertheless, where the same episodes are illustrated, the diagnostic features remain consistent from the tenth to the thirteenth centuries, and it is only these which can form the criteria for identification. The diagnostic features have been defined on the basis of the 'developed' pictorial and literary forms of the story, the Ramsund carving, the Norwegian portals and the Eddaic poems (with certain variations in Vǫlsunga saga). Diagnostic features of the chief 'units' or episodes are in brief as follows:

Sigurðr scenes (not all these elements need be present): the association with the smith who forges a sword for the hero; the killing of Fáfnir from beneath; the roasting of Fáfnir's heart by a thumb-sucking Sigurðr; the birds who warn Sigurðr of the smith's treachery; the horse on to which the dragon's treasure is piled.

Gunnarr scenes: a bound figure playing the harp with his toes, surrounded by snakes.

In the following I take each period and region in turn and classify the various illustrations as certain, probable or possible, and quite uncertain representations of elements of the Vǫlsung story.

I. Fifth to ninth centuries

The claim that figures on the bracteates of the fifth to the seventh centuries represent the thumb-sucking Sigurðr and Gunnarr in the snake-enclosure has been disputed.[3] The figures are highly stylised and little is sufficiently individual to establish a particular iconography. The fact that the figure with the raised hand and prominent thumb and the figure surrounded by snakes are

---

[2] A. M. Franzén, "Odens öga", *Fornvännen* LIII (1958), 195-8.

[3] J. J. A. Worsaae, "Om forestillingerne paa guldbracteaterne", *Aarbøger for nordisk Oldkyndighed og Historie* (1870), 382-419. Disputed by M. Mackeprang, *De nordiske guldbrakteater* (1952), 88-95. See also A. Jorn, *Indfald og udfald* (1972), figs. 175-7.

usually only shown as busts indicates their origin in the portraits of Roman emperors on medallions, which the bracteates imitated.

The literary/historical archetypes of Sigurðr and Gunnarr (if they existed at all) may belong to this period but our knowledge of the form of the legend at this stage is too hazy to give any support to these identifications.

The figure on the front of the Oseberg cart has been identified as Gunnarr in the snake-enclosure,[4] which would give a date of about 800 for the earliest pictorial account of the legend. However, distinctive elements such as the bound hands and the harp are absent. The figure is spread-eagled and grasps snakes with both hands, the posture emphatically unlike the typical Gunnarr stance in the later representations. The attributes and posture are, however, similar to the image of the man between two beasts, a common enough image in Scandinavian art from the Migration period onwards which seems to represent the more general theme of a hero's struggle with death.

A number of other early 'Gunnarr' scenes can be dismissed for similar reasons; these occur on brooches[5] and on picture stones on Gotland.[6] None of the motifs on the brooches are precise enough to imply a particular narrative. The picture stones in question, though probably decorated with narrative material, have only doubtful associations with the Vǫlsung legend.

II. Late Viking Age illustrations
Tenth and eleventh centuries

The Isle of Man

Four cross-slabs decorated with Vǫlsung illustrations (two possible scenes among them) survive on the Isle of Man.

[4] H. Shetelig *et al., Osebergfundet* (1917-28), III 27-46, pl. V, fig. 19. Most other books on the Viking Age make the same identification.

[5] B. Nerman, "Man och Orm. En bildframställning på en grupp gotländska spännen från sen vendeltid", *Fornvännen* L (1955), 191-4; J. Anderson, "Notes on relics of the Viking period of the Northmen in Scotland", *Proceedings of the Society of Antiquaries of Scotland* X (1872-4), 536-94; J. Graham-Campbell, "The Viking-age silver and gold hoards of Scandinavian character from Scotland", *Proceedings of the Society of Antiquaries of Scotland*, CVII (1975-6), 114-35.

[6] *Picture stones with snake-enclosures:* Klinte Hunninge I, Ardre VIII, see S. Lindqvist, *Gotlands Bildsteine* (1941-2), figs. 128 & 139. See also phallic figure grasping snakes shown on Aspö stone at Lagnö, Södermanland, E. Brate & E. Wessén, *Södermanlands runinskrifter* (1924-36), pl. LXXXIV. *Picture stones with some similar elements to the Vǫlsung legend illustrations:* bound man with one leg fettered in bottom left of field and seated figure in centre with raised hand holding a ?ring with an? anvil in front on Ardre III, see S. Lindqvist, *op. cit.,* fig. 169. Running figure in profile with a raised hand and prominent thumb, below, a standing figure with arms looped around two flanking serpents on Ardre V, see S. Lindqvist, *op. cit.,* fig. 164.

Fig. 1. Cross-slab at Kirk Andreas, Isle of Man

Kirk Andreas (no. 121): This tenth-century stone shows the dragon Fáfnir as a serpent (lying vertically because of demands of space) being killed by Sigurðr, a half-length figure in profile (Fig. 1). Above, Sigurðr roasts Fáfnir's heart on a spit with his thumb in his mouth (tasting Fáfnir's blood and thus understanding the warnings of the birds about the treachery of Reginn the smith). Above him are the heads of his horse Grani and of a bird. The figure with bound hands and feet on the reverse may represent Gunnarr in the snake-enclosure (Fig. 2) but since there is no harp we cannot count this as a

Fig. 2. Cross-slab at Kirk Andreas, Isle of Man

certain identification. The presence of Sigurðr scenes on the other face, however, makes a Gunnarr scene at least plausible.

Malew (no. 120): the very worn stone (now in the gallery of the church) shows the killing of Fáfnir, depicted in the same way as on the Kirk Andreas stone, but with an additional feature (Fig. 3). There is a semicircular line between Sigurðr and the dragon, perhaps indicating the pit from which, according to the prose of *Fáfnismál,* Sigurðr killed Fáfnir. Because of the placing of the figure and the semicircular line, the iconographic effect is the

Fig.3 Cross-slab at Malew, Isle of Man   Fig. 4. Cross-slab at Jurby, Isle of Man

same as if the figure were placed beneath the body of the dragon, a distinctive element of this particular episode. Above, Sigurðr roasts the heart; though badly worn, the raised hand and the horizontal spit can be seen.

Jurby (no. 119): the killing of Fáfnir is depicted in the same way as on the Malew stone, with the semicircular line indicating the pit. Sigurðr is shown as a small figure in profile (Fig. 4).

Maughold (no. 122): the early eleventh-century slab found at Ramsey and now in Maughold churchyard (Fig. 5) shows an otter with a fish in its mouth, possibly a representation of one of the earliest episodes in the legend, in which Otr, eating a salmon, is killed by Loki who walks by with the gods Óðinn and Hoenir. Beside the otter with the fish, a seated figure may represent Sigurðr

Fig. 5. Cross-slab at Maughold (from Ramsey), Isle of Man

Fig. 6. Churchyard cross at Halton, Lancashire, England

holding the spit, shown as a diagonal feature in the centre of the slab, with slices of heart on it. There is a horse above. The carving is so stylised that no certain identification can be made.

The north of England

There is only one well-defined scene illustrating the Volsung legend in this region.

Halton, Lancashire: three scenes are shown on the east face of a cross-shaft in the churchyard of Halton church (Fig. 6). The smith is shown in the largest panel at the base of the shaft, surrounded by the tools of his trade. Above,

Fig. 7. Figure on cross-head from Ripon cathedral, Yorkshire, England

Sigurðr is shown standing in profile with raised hand (and probably the thumb in his mouth), holding a horizontal spit; in the panel above, two birds in a bush. A group of monuments in the north of England have recently been identified by James Lang.[7] Of these only two, the *Ripon* cross-head found in the north transept of the Cathedral and the *York* grave-slab (from grave 7 in the south transept of the Minster), can be afforded any credence. The crouching figure on the Ripon cross-head (Fig. 7) may well have affinities with orants or devotees in similar positions on Celtic crosses[8] so that any similarities with the seated Sigurðr roasting the dragon's heart must be qualified by the possibility of another ancestry. It is also possible that a couple of prototypes have merged to produce this figure. I believe the decoration of the York slab should be seen as reflecting a repertoire of Scandinavian taste but not necessarily depicting the story in its classic form. On the edge of the slab (Fig. 8) a running figure wields a sword between two serpents, possibly related to a scene of Sigurðr killing Fáfnir; on one face there appears to be a figure and a tree, which James Lang has identified as a heart-roasting scene.

[7] J. Lang, "Sigurd Fafnesbane og Vølund Smed. Nogle nordengelske stenbilleder", *Den Iconographiske Post* (1974 pt. 3), 13-24; "En ny Sigurd", *Den Iconographiske Post* (1975 pt. 2-3), 47-8; "Sigurd and Weland in pre-Conquest carving from northern England", *Yorkshire Archaeological Journal* XLVIII (1976), 83-94; "The sculptors of the Nunburnholme cross", *The Archaeological Journal* CXXXIII (1976), 75-94; Appendix II in R.A. Hall, "Rescue excavations in the crypt of Ripon cathedral", *Yorkshire Archaeological Journal* XLIX (1977), 59-63.

[8] See the cross of SS Patrick and Columba at Kells, J. Romilly Allen, *Early Christian symbolism in Great Britain and Ireland before the thirteenth century* (1887), fig. 34. A useful analogy is the eighth-century cross from Drumhallagh, Donegal on which there are two crouching figures each with thumb in mouth, identified by Henry as a confusion between weeping angels and a traditional figure of Finn-mac-Coul, F. Henry, *Irish Art in the early Christian period to 800 AD* (1965), fig. 15a.

Fig. 8. Part of decoration on
edge of grave-slab from the
Minster, York, England

The other monuments in the group are decorated with scenes which not only lack the distinctive features of the Vǫlsung legend but which (in one case at least) can also be identified as something else altogether. The scene on one face of the *Heysham* hog-back, with a tree, a quadruped, a man with raised hands and birds is more likely to be a simple hunt-scene, like the one on the other face. On one panel of the *Nunburnholme* cross in Yorkshire, two small seated figures (added by a second sculptor below a large figure apparently holding a chalice) are more likely to be Saint Antony and Saint Paul in the desert, than Sigurðr and Reginn. The saints were traditionally shown breaking bread between them, a symbol of the Mass and therefore entirely fitting to accompany the priest with the chalice above. The scene on the shaft built into the south wall of the nave of *Kirby Hill* church in Yorkshire is so disjointed as to be 'illegible' iconographically: a headless body, a figure with a raised hand and an ?anvil.

Sweden
Four well-defined scenes remain.

Ramsund, Södermanland (Fig. 9): a carving on natural rock shows Sigurðr killing from beneath the serpent Fáfnir, actually the rune band; there is the headless body of the decapitated smith, Reginn; Sigurðr is seated with his thumb to his mouth and the entire heart of Fáfnir on a stick over a flame; Grani bearing the treasure-chest is tied to a tree in which two birds are perched.

Gök, Södermanland (Fig. 10): most of the same motifs occur but crudely drawn and totally disjointed as if the Ramsund model had been copied without

Fig. 9. Carving on natural rock at Ramsund, Södermanland, Sweden

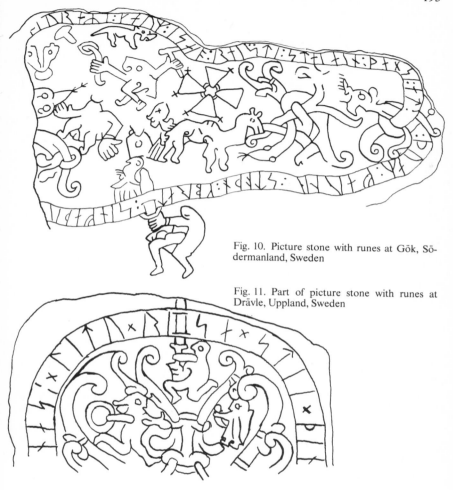

Fig. 10. Picture stone with runes at Gök, Södermanland, Sweden

Fig. 11. Part of picture stone with runes at Drävle, Uppland, Sweden

understanding. For instance, the tree has developed a serpent's head and the bird no longer perches in it.

Drävle, Uppland (Fig. 11): as on the Ramsund carving, the killing of Fáfnir is represented by Sigurðr piercing the rune band with his sword. Below, the pair of confronted figures, one a female with a drinking-horn, the other a male with a ring, no doubt represent Sigurðr wooing Sigrdrífa as told in the prose passages of *Sigrdrífomál:* on being awoken by Sigurðr, Sigrdrífa offers him a drinking-horn full of mead.

Ramsjö, Uppland (Fig. 12): this is such a poor and almost illegible copy of the Drävle scheme that the runes are merely imitation runes!

Three other rune stones have been included in the corpus, all from Gästrikland. The *Årsunda* scene (Fig. 13) may be a crude rendering of the Drävle/-Ramsjö wooing scene though there is only one figure with a ?ring, and the 'warrior' has no sword. Though a similar pair of confronted figures appears in the bottom of the field on the Ockelbo stone (now lost), other motifs do not seem to relate to the Vǫlsung legend. The same is the case with the Österfärnebo stone (also lost).

Norway

No certain, probable or possible scenes survive from this period in Norway. Three eleventh century Ringerike-style monuments however have been included in the corpus. All three are now in the Oldsaksamling in Oslo.

The impressive *Alstad* stone from Oppland has been said to show the return of the riderless Grani with Gunnarr and Hǫgni on horseback, who killed Sigurðr while out hunting[9] according to the German sources of the legend. It is more likely to be a hunting-scene, since the literary sources supporting the identification are all much later than the stone itself.

The *Tanberg* stone from Buskerud (Fig. 14) has been classified by Fuglesang in her corpus of Ringerike-style monuments as a trial-piece and this has, I think, important implications for the iconography. It is quite simply unfinished and there is nothing to indicate whether a figure was ever intended to wield the sword or if so, what the wielder's identity would have been. The Vǫlsung iconography was undoubtedly well known and popular but it is doubtful what intention an artist/iconographer would have had in producing such cryptic illustrations.

The *Gran* stone from Oppland was tentatively included in the exhibition catalogue.[10] The case for the smith's tools incised on it (bellows, anvil, tongs, forge stone and flames) being Reginn's is quite untenable. There are no distinctive features and no reason why smiths' tools should represent Reginn's in particular: tools were sometimes shown on monuments marking the graves of smiths.[11] The identification of motifs on fragments should in any case be treated with extreme caution.

---

[9] L. Jacobsen, *Evje-stenen og Alstad-stenen* (1933), 30ff.

[10] M. Blindheim and E. Hohler, *op. cit., 19, 30.*

[11] J. Vellev, "Hammer og tang", *Skalk* (1975 pt. 4), 25-30.

Fig. 12. Part of picture stone with runes at Ramsjö, Uppland, Sweden

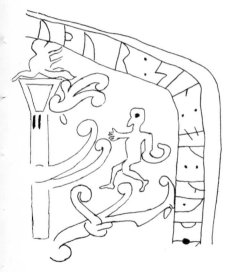

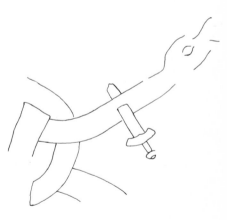

Fig. 13. Part of picture stone with runes at Årsunda, Gästrikland, Sweden

Fig. 14. Part of decoration on picture stone fragment from Tanberg, Buskerud, Norway

III Romanesque illustrations
Twelfth and thirteenth centuries.

Norway

Well-defined cycles of scenes survive on portals from five stave churches in southern Norway: the late twelfth-century portals from the churches of Hylestad, Vegusdal and Austad in Aust-Agder, and the thirteenth-century portal from Lardal in Vestfold (all these portals now in the Oldsaksamling in Oslo) and the thirteenth-century portal from Mael in Upper Telemark, now in the Tinn and Rjukan Museum.

Hylestad (reading the scenes from the bottom of the right-hand jamb upwards): we see Reginn the smith in his smithy with a helper operating the bellows (only in *Vǫlsunga saga* is there mention of the lads in the smithy[12]) (Fig. 15). In the medallion above, Sigurðr is shown in the right of the field testing the sword which Reginn forged for him (Fig. 16); the sword was not strong enough for the hero, who broke it asunder on the anvil (also a variation on the main theme found only in *Vǫlsunga saga*[13]). Above, Sigurðr kneels in the pit represented by the medallion frame to kill Fáfnir from below (Fig. 17). On the left-hand jamb (from the bottom upwards): Sigurðr roasts Fáfnir's heart in slices on a spit, with his thumb in his mouth (Fig. 18). Opposite him, Reginn sleeps, his head resting on the pommel of his sword. Above, three birds perch in the branches of a tree; once Fáfnir's blood touches his lips, Sigurðr understands their warnings that Reginn is plotting to kill him. Beside the tree is the horse Grani (Fig. 19), loaded with Fáfnir's treasure for which Reginn had lusted, and which originally Loki had stolen from the dwarf Andvari to pay atonement for the death of Otr, the brother of Reginn and Fáfnir. In the scene above, Sigurðr plunges his sword through Reginn's chest (Fig. 20). At the top of the jamb (so far as it survives today) is a scene from the end of the legend showing Gunnarr in the snake-enclosure (Fig. 21) (into which he was thrown by King Atli, also lusting after the treasure), playing the lyre with his toes. This unusual method of performing upon the lyre is first mentioned in *Atlamál* of the late twelfth century, that is, contemporary with these pictures. The image may be the responsibility of an iconographer since a more literal approach is needed in order to express in iconographic terms the heroic death of Gunnarr bound in a snake-enclosure playing the harp (as first told in *Atlakviða* of the early tenth century). As we shall see, this episode was enormously popular on its own.

---

[12] R. G. Finch, ed. *Vǫlsunga saga. The saga of the Volsungs* (1965), 27.
[13] *Ibid.*, 27.

Fig. 15. Portal from Hylestad stave church, Aust-Agder, Norway

Fig. 16. Portal from Hylestad stave church, Aust-Agder, Norway

Sue Margeson

Fig. 17. Portal from Hylestad stave church, Aust-Agder, Norway

Fig. 18. Portal from Hylestad stave church, Aust-Agder, Norway

Fig. 19. Portal from Hylestad stave church, Aust-Agder, Norway

Fig. 20. Portal from Hylestad stave church, Aust-Agder, Norway

Fig. 21. Portal from Hylestad stave church, Aust-Agder, Norway

Fig. 22. Portal from Vegusdal stave church, Aust-Agder, Norway

Vegusdal (Fig. 22): there is no doubt that the four scenes in medallions on the left-hand jamb illustrate some of the same episodes as on the Hylestad portal but there is no narrative sequence and even within medallions there is some confusion. From top to bottom we see the killing of Reginn; the testing of the sword (confused with the horse and the treasure-chest; furthermore, the horse has its hoof up on the anvil as if being shod, as though not two but three scenes have been confused here); and the roasting of the heart. Though the lay-out is similar to the Hylestad portal, the work is clearly by a different hand.

Austad: the scene at the base of the left-hand jamb shows Gunnarr in the snake-enclosure (Fig. 23), a scene owing much to the Hylestad model but which has an additional figure holding two circular objects. It has been suggested that the standing figure may be Atli trying to discover from Gunnarr the hiding-place of the treasure. It is perhaps more likely that it is a condensed pictorial reference to a passage in *Atlakviða*[14] in which Gunnarr compares the hearts of Hjalli the coward and of Hǫgni: when he asks for the heart of his brother Hǫgni, Atli tries to fool him with the heart of the thrall Hjalli but Gunnarr recognises it instantly. On the right-hand jamb, the cutting out of Hǫgni's heart is represented (Fig. 24).

Lardal (reading from top to bottom of the right-hand jamb): a warrior with his shield (?Sigurðr); the otter-skin spread out over pellets representing gold, with Andvari's cursed ring round the neck (the earliest, and one of only two representations of the otter atonement) (Fig. 25); Reginn in his smithy; Fáfnir; Sigurðr seated and holding two swords (Fig. 26), one of which he plunges from beneath into the belly of the dragon. The other, held downwards, perhaps indicates a second episode conflated with the first, namely the cutting out of Fáfnir's heart which according to *Vǫlsunga saga*[15] was done by Sigurðr with a second sword.

Mael: from top to bottom, the scenes in medallions begin with ?Sigurðr; the otter skin stretched over gold as on the Lardal portal; Reginn in his smithy; Fáfnir (this medallion has been damaged due to re-use of the planks as floorboards in the mid-nineteenth century); Sigurðr with one sword raised to plunge into Fáfnir, and a second sword held just above the horizontal as if in use, again suggesting reference to the cutting out of Fáfnir's heart. Below, the horse Grani is shown carrying a treasure-chest.

Well-defined single scenes occur on the base of a door-jamb from the twelfth-century church at Nes in Telemark and on a capital (now in private

---

[14] *Atlakviða*, st. 23, 25, G. Neckel, H. Kuhn, ed. *Edda*...I. Text (1965), 244.
[15] *Ed. cit. Vǫlsunga saga* (1965), 33-4.

Fig. 23 Portal from Austad stave church, Aust-Agder, Norway

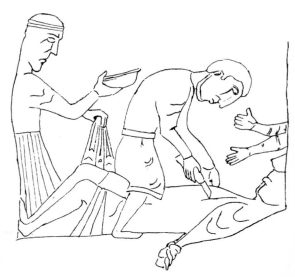

Fig. 24. Portal from Austad stave church, Aust-Agder, Norway

Fig. 26. Portal from Lardal stave church, Vestfold, Norway

Fig. 25. Portal from Lardal stave church, Vestfold, Norway

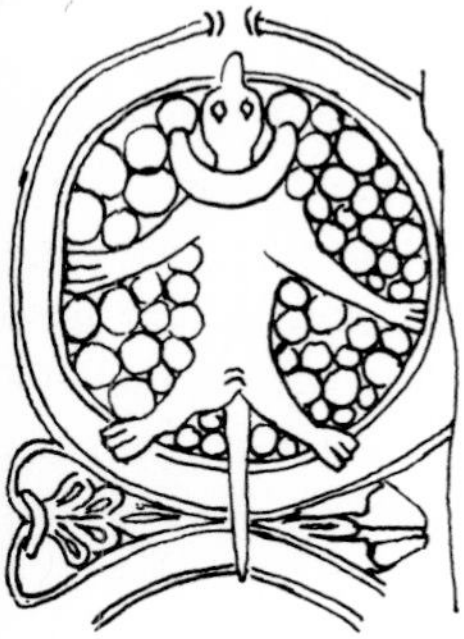

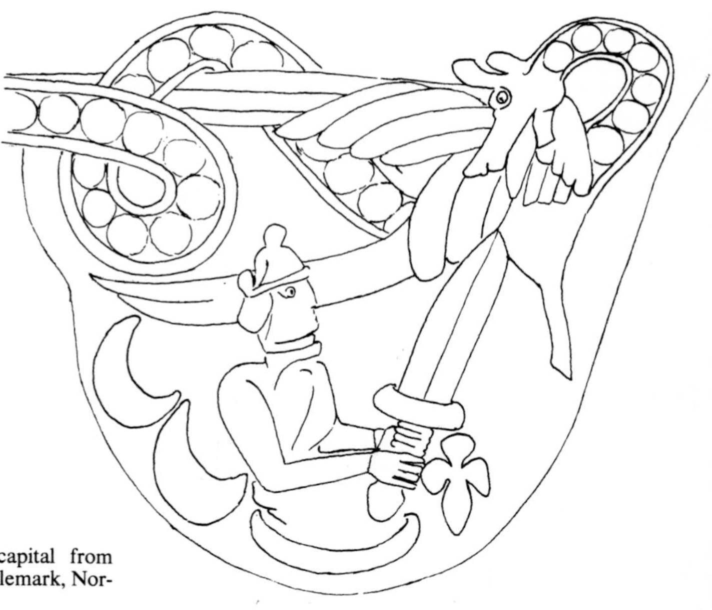

Fig. 27. Marble capital from
Lunde church, Telemark, Norway

ownership) from the demolished church at Lunde nearby (Fig. 27): the scene shows the dragon Fáfnir being killed from below by Sigurðr from one of three holes represented by crescents in low relief. This latter variation occurs in literature only in *Vǫlsunga saga.*[16]

A standing Gunnarr in a snake-enclosure, playing the lyre with his toes, is shown on the thirteenth-century bench from *Heddal* church in Telemark (now in Gol stave church at the Folk Museum in Oslo); on a drinking-horn from *Mo* in Telemark (Fig. 28) and on a doorway at *Uvdal* stave church in Numedal (in this case, he is shown playing a harp not a lyre).

There is a possible illustration of the wooing of Brynhildr by Sigurðr and Gunnarr on the back of a chair in *Heddal* church in Telemark (Fig. 29): a central figure on a ?mound is flanked by two horsemen, one holding a ring.

There are a number of scenes which have come to be associated with the Vǫlsung legend but which do not stand up to closer examination. A damaged and altered door-jamb from *Nesland* stave church in Telemark (now inside a newer church there) is decorated with several medallions, a scheme obviously based on the well-known cycles from Aust-Agder and Vestfold. Two of the medallions (Fig. 30) contain figures previously identified as Loki and Andvari[17] but which are clearly based on misunderstood ecclesiastical prototypes: the uppermost is in a kirtle with a stole over one shoulder (deacon's stoles are worn in this manner); both arms are raised, and he holds a chalice to his ear; the round object by his other hand is no doubt a paten since the prototype must have been a priest celebrating Mass. In the medallion below, a similar figure wearing a stole holds two small circular objects in raised hands, presumably the wafers of the Host. The arc behind the figure suggests confusion with yet another scene: Christ in glory seated on a rainbow. In the medallion at the bottom of the jamb as it survives there is a horse carrying a chest which may have been based on a Grani prototype but even if this is the case it is not reason enough to identify the figures above as illustrating the Vǫlsung legend.

Several dragon-killing scenes come into this category: one of the side panels of the Blaker gård chair now in the Oldsaksamling; the Heddal desk (now in a house in the Folk Museum) and the Gudbrandsdal box (also in the Folk

---

[16] *Ibid.,* 30.

[17] M. Blindheim and E. Hohler, *op. cit.* 25; M. Blindheim *op. cit.* 12-13. Previously, Berge had also identified them as Loki and Andvari; alternatively the first 'ecclesiastic' was Sigurðr drinking the magic drink given him by Grimhildr to make him forget Brynhildr and marry Guðrún, and the second Sigurðr going through the flames to woo Brynhildr on behalf of Gunnarr! See R. Berge, *Vinje og Rauland* (1940), I 258-62.

Fig. 28. Motif on drinking-horn from Mo, Telemark, Norway

Fig. 29. Back of chair in Heddal stave church, Telemark, Norway

Fig. 30. Portal from Nesland stave church, Telemark, Norway

Fig. 31. Part of one side of font from Norum, Bohuslän, Sweden

Museum collections); a door-jamb of a store-house at Lundeval farm in Telemark. None of these have any diagnostic motifs to associate them with the story of Sigurðr Fáfnisbani.

Sweden

Two well-defined scenes of Gunnarr in the snake-enclosure survive from areas of Sweden which were part of Norway in the Middle Ages. The twelfth-century stone font from Norum in Bohuslän (Fig. 31) and a pine font of the early thirteenth century from Näs in Jämtland. On the latter, Gunnarr is shown seated with his legs intertwined with the harp strings in a most impractical manner!

There is no time here to consider any more of the so-called Vǫlsung illustrations, suffice it to say that scenes have been identified as far afield as Russia and Spain, and that in my opinion none of them can be classified as certain, though one or two might fall into the 'possible' category.

IV Discussion

Once the well-defined pictures have been distinguished from the more doubtful material, and a more critical distribution has been established, we can begin to look at the information actually offered by the pictures. Perhaps most important is the way in which the iconography complements the extant literature.

We know that several linked episodes of the Vǫlsung legend were current in the tenth century as shown by the Manx crosses, though there are only fragmentary references in the very scanty literature we have of such early date. In particular, the motif of the otter, represented eating a fish on the Maughold cross-slab, does not occur in literature until the prose of *Reginsmál* (twelfth or thirteenth century, while the verse is thought to be of the eleventh century). It is found in a catalogue stanza attributed to *Bjarkamál* which is difficult to date but is more likely to be twelfth/thirteenth century than tenth/eleventh. Thereafter, the otter is illustrated only on the thirteenth-century portals from the stave churches of Lardal in Vestfold and Mael in Telemark. There it is explicitly the otter-geld, the skin spread over the gold with Andvaranautr around the neck.

The Swedish rune stones with pictures in Södermanland and Uppland indicate the currency of the Vǫlsung legend in the East Norse area though no literature on the subject survives there.

Similarly, the Vǫlsung iconography in Norway testifies to the popularity of the legend there though most of the literary sources are Icelandic.

Some variations in the Norwegian pictures occur in literature only in *Vǫlsunga saga:* for example, Reginn in his smithy with a helper (on the Hylestad portal), the forging of more than one sword by Reginn for the hero (shown on Hylestad), Sigurðr's killing of Fáfnir from one of several pits (shown on the capital from Lunde church and the base of a door-jamb at Nes church in Telemark). These correspondences add weight to the idea that *Vǫlsunga saga* was probably composed in Norway.

Moving away from the problems of identification, I want now to consider interpretation. Much scholarly energy has been expended on arguing whether these pictures are pagan or Christian.

My view is that given the degree of overlap between the pagan and the Christian in the late Viking Age (see the often cited parallels between Þórr's hammer and the cross, for example), it is hardly feasible to categorise the tenth and eleventh-century material as pagan, let alone that of the twelfth and thirteenth centuries. Many of the late Viking illustrations occur on memorial stones and must have been intended to glorify the memory of the dead man by drawing analogies with the deeds of heroes. The Romanesque illustrations cannot be explained merely as the result of a retrogressive Norwegian Church looking back to its pagan origins, since the church-carvings belong to at least a tributary of Romanesque art in Europe.[18] There is no time here to discuss the thorny problems of stylistic affiliations but it seems likely that the east coast of England (Yorkshire, Lincolnshire and East Anglia) must have provided many impulses; trading links with these areas were particularly close. It is clear from the literary evidence that the Vǫlsung legend in the twelfth and thirteenth centuries was not a subject for conservative or isolated wood-carvers in the depths of Telemark and Aust-Agder. This just happens to be where the iconography survives. The Vǫlsung legend was well known in cultivated circles in the West Norse area, Iceland and Norway. Kings expected their skalds to be familiar with the legend. For instance, King Haraldr Harðráði commanded his skald Þióðólfr to compose a poem on a quarrel between a tanner and a blacksmith in terms of Sigurðr's fight with Fáfnir, stipulating that his kennings should refer to their trades. Þióðólfr's poem earned him a gold finger-ring.[19]

The skald Þorfinnr is asked by King Óláfr to compose a poem on the decoration of tapestries hanging in the hall. His poem tells of the killing of Fáfnir by Sigurðr and there are some indications in the verse (for example, the references to colour) that he actually knew a pictorial version.[20]

The fact that the story of Sigurðr was known in such circles is entirely in keeping with what we know of skaldic verse and its repertoire. The Vǫlsung legend had in the tenth and eleventh centuries become part of a common stock of vocabulary and imagery available to poets. The *Skáldskaparmál* in Snorri's *Edda* shows that in the early thirteenth century there was a deliberate attempt to keep alive traditional stories and traditional modes of expression. The Vǫlsung legend is related by Snorri in explanation of a series of kennings for gold: why gold is called otter's atonement *(otrgiǫld)*, the burden of Grani *(byrðr Grana);* the Niflungs inheritance *(Niflunga arfr)*.

Cultivated circles were, on the one hand, eager to absorb European fashions in architecture and the decorative arts; and on the other, eager to retain their native traditions. The 'court' fostered composition of sagas such as *Vǫlsunga saga* which can be seen as a product of this antiquarian revival. Landowners in

---

[18] For the most detailed recent discussion of problems of stave-church dating, see P. Anker, "Om dateringsproblemet i stavkirkeforskningen", *Historisk Tidsskrift* (1977 pt. 2), 103-42.

[19] F. Jónsson, ed. *Morkinskinna* (1932), 235-6.

[20] G. Vigfusson, C. R. Unger, ed. *Flateyjarbók* (1860-68), III 244.

country areas responsible for the building of churches (though by this stage no longer the owners of churches) evidently sought to have them decorated in a manner reflecting this royal taste.

The iconography of the Vǫlsung legend was obviously acceptable to the church authorities. It does not appear to have had any allegorical significance, however. It is advisable to remember at this stage that the present distribution of Sigurðr iconography is only the result of accidents of survival and that virtually nothing remains in the secular context, such as house-furnishings and vessels, the very area where literary references lead us to suppose a widespread pictorial tradition existed, but which of course is more subject to damage and wear and tear. The Mo drinking-horn is the only secular object to have survived decorated with this story. We must beware of giving an exaggerated significance to the appearance of heroic material on church doorways and furnishings.

There is another important element in the twelfth-century view of its hero which emphasises the lack of symbolism in the Vǫlsung illustrations. The story of Sigurðr was given a degree of historical authenticity as shown by references in the twelfth-century *Leiðarvísir,* an Icelandic guide-book for pilgrims to Rome and beyond. Gnitaheiðr where Sigurðr killed Fáfnir and the place where Gunnarr died in the snake-enclosure are both mentioned here.[21]

Another such example is the reference in the *Lǫgmannsannáll* under the year 1405 to the finding of the hilt of Sigurðr's sword in Germany:[22] rather superhuman history, it is true, since the sword is ten feet long!

Even in the literary accounts with ostensibly a more moralistic tone, there is no indication of a rigid 'moral' framework constructed around the so-called pagan hero Sigurðr.

Such is the case with the story of Þorsteinn[23] who visited a 22-seater privy at midnight only to discover the dark figure of a spirit from hell seated at the far end. Þorsteinn asks him who best endures the torments of hell. The spirit's reply that Sigurðr Fáfnisbani does seems to evoke the image of the triumphant hero rather than the punished sinner. The dialogue proceeds with a sense of the comic and the moralistic tone is rather diluted by the obvious delight in the story itself and its sinister humour.

In *Nornagests Þáttr,* we find a similar enjoyment as opposed to moral fervour. After hearing of the deeds of Sigurðr, the King's followers enjoy the

[21] K. Kålund, ed. *Alfrædi íslenzk* (1908-18), I 13, 16.

[22] G. Jónsson, ed. *Annálar og Nafnaskrá* (1948), 142.

[23] *Ed. cit., Flateyjarbók,* I 416.

story of Brynhildr's journey to Hel and her abode. When they ask for more, the King stops Gestr's tale and asks him to tell of Ragnarr Loðbrók instead.[24] It is their enjoyment which apparently provokes the King's rebuke but if the episode was intended to present the stern image of the missionary king, his reaction is extremely casual and does not carry any moral weight. In fact a moment before, caught up in the story himself, the King asked how Sigurðr died.

In only one instance is there direct disapproval of the hero. In the saga of St Óláfr, the Saint rebukes his poet Sigvatr in a dream for using a refrain from the *Sigurðar saga* in the poem Sigvatr composed in his honour. He suggests the use of a more appropriate refrain from *Genesis*.[25] This rebuke is entirely in keeping with the nature of the saga of a missionary king, unlike the previous example.

In literature, the heroes Sigurðr and Gunnarr are not seen as part of any moral framework nor as part of any allegorical scheme, they appear as neither damned pagans nor as Christian heroes, though it is possible that their deeds were related in a general way to the theme of good fighting evil in the shape of dragon and serpents.

This seems to me to have direct bearing on interpreting the carvings. I suggest that the judgement passed by the author of *Vǫlsunga saga* on Sigurðr's place in popular memory probably reflects the nature of Sigurðr's appeal to the craftsman and to his patron and audience alike. It is said that Sigurðr's name 'would never be forgotten where German was spoken nor yet in the Northern lands, as long as the world endured'. Given the amount of scholarly interest aroused by the Vǫlsung illustrations, the author was a more accurate prophet than he knew!

Castle Museum, Norwich

---

[24] *Ibid.*, I 355-7.
[25] *Ibid.*, II 394.

Members and associate members of the Symposium

Jens Peter Ægidius
Brynjulf Alver
Aagot Andersen
Flemming G. Andersen
Hanne Bønløkke Andersen
Lise Præstgaard Andersen
Det Arnamagnæanske Institut,
  København
Karen Ascani
Knud Banning
Lisbeth Baumgarten
Heinrich Beck
Lise Bek
Hans Bekker-Nielsen
M. Berg-Sonne
Merete Blomberg
Hans Blosen
Benedicte Bojesen
Giovanni Battista Bronzini
Wolfgang Brückner
Peter Buchholz
Gunilla Byrman
Marianne Novrup Børch
Anny Bøttger
Hans Henrik Bøttger
Birte Carlé
Michael Chesnutt
Anker Clausen

Christoph Daxelmüller
Dialekt- och Folkminnesarkivet
  Uppsala
Ruth Dinesen
Marian Ege
Harald Ehrhardt
Dorrit Einersen
Sigrid Engeler
Bent Fausing
Hans Jørgen Frederiksen
Francois Garnier
Stefanie Gropper
Olaf Grunert
Uffe Grøn
Angela Guski
Andreas Haarder
Kirsten Haarder
Ulla Haastrup
Jan Ragner Hagland
Eyvind Fjeld Halvorsen
Birgit Hansen
Háskólabókasafn, Reykjavik
J. Fredrik Heinemann
H. M. Heinrichs
Wilhelm Heizmann
Thorbjörg Helgadottir
Kristine Heltberg
Svend Hendrup

Gustav Henningsen
Gun Herranen
Michael Herslund
Tage Hind
Bjarne Hodne
Dietrich Hoffmann
Inge Holzapfel
Otto Holzapfel
Shaun F. D. Hughes
Jógvan S. Høgnesen
Lilliane Højgaard
Kirsten Bech Hørby
Institut for Kunsthistorie,
  København
Eric Jacobsen
Dorte Skovgaard Jensen
Helle Jensen
Jytte Jensen
Povl Johs. Jensen
Søren Skovgaard Jensen
Kerstin Louise Johansson
Arne Odd Johnsen
Jørgen Højgaard Jørgensen
Søren Kaspersen
A. M. Kinghorn
Jonna Kjær
Else Marie Kofod
Inger-Lise Kolstrup
Reimund Kvideland
Sigurd Kværndrup
Eugenia de Lamotte
Wibke Rickers Larsen
Karin Lidell
Louise Lilie
Fl. Lundgreen-Nielsen
Ole Lund-Hansen
Dora Maček

Susan Margeson
Eske K. Mathiesen
Julia McGrew
Brian Patrick McGuire
J. S. McKinnell
R. W. McTurk
Jørn Moestrup
Else Mundal
Marina Mundt
Xenia Muratova
Hans Frede Nielsen
Søren Noe-Nygaard
Nordisk Institutt, Bergen
Tore Nyberg
Ebbe Nyborg
Esther Nyholm
Thorhildur Oddsdottir
Thorkild Damsgaard Olsen
Teresa Paroli
D. A. Pearsall
Birthe Marie Pedersen
Rita Pedersen
Viggo Hjørnager Pedersen
Inge Petersen
Iørn Piø
Marianne Powell
Sv. E. Præstholm
Alex Quaade
Julie Randlev
Gunnar Jacob Ries
Sixten Ringbom
Eva Rode
Hanne Ruus
Margit Lave Rønsholt
Elisabeth Salter
Sanghistorisk Arkiv, Århus
Kurt Schier

Jens Peter Schjødt
Kirsten Schottländer
Reinhold Schröder
Lene Schøsler
Hubert Seelow
Birgitte Seider
T. A. Shippey
Svavar Sigmundsson
Aldís Sigurdardóttir
Claus Beck Skadhauge
Inge Skovgaard-Petersen
Henrik Specht
Peter Springborg
James Stewart
Carl Stief
Flemming Talbo Stubkjær
Preben Meulengracht Sørensen
Arnfinnur Thomasen
Allan Thomsen
Marie-Louise Thomsen
Sverrir Tómasson
Aage Trommer
Tor Ulset
Universität des Saarlandes,
    Saarbrücken
Elisabeth Vestergaard
Elsebeth Vinten
Hans-Uwe Vollertsen
Mette Wad
Erik Koed Westergaard
Westf. Wilhelms-Universität,
    Münster
Carla del Zotto
Österreichisches Museum für
    Volkskunde, Wien

Oral Tradition – Literary Tradition. A Symposium: Edited by Hans Bekker-Nielsen, Peter Foote, Andreas Haarder, Hans Frede Nielsen. Odense: Odense University Press, 1977. 121 pp.

The European Medieval Ballad. A Symposium. Edited by Otto Holzapfel in collaboration with Julia McGrew and Iørn Piø. Odense: Odense University Press, 1978. 121 pp.

Hans Frede Nielsen, *De germanske sprog. Baggrund og gruppering.* Odense: Odense Universitetsforlag, 1979. 130 pp.

Medieval Narrative. A Symposium. Edited by Hans Bekker-Nielsen, Peter Foote, Andreas Haarder, Preben Meulengracht Sørensen. Odense: Odense University Press, 1979. 139 pp.

Otto Holzapfel, *Det balladeske. Fortællemåden i den ældre episke folkevise.* Odense: Odense Universitetsforlag, 1980. 122 pp.

Preben Meulengracht Sørensen, *Norrønt nid.* Odense: Odense Universitetsforlag, 1980. 135 pp.

DATE DUE